KU-597-321

# THE PARISH COMES ALIVE

BY

E. W. SOUTHCOTT

*Vicar of St. Wilfrid's Church, Halton, Leeds*
*and Canon of Ripon Cathedral*

LONDON

A. R. MOWBRAY & Co. Limited

First published in 1956
Fourth impression, 1961

PRINTED IN GREAT BRITAIN BY
A. R. MOWBRAY & CO. LIMITED IN THE CITY OF OXFORD
1340

DEDICATED TO

THE BISHOP OF RIPON

THE BISHOP OF KNARESBOROUGH

MY COLLEAGUES, PAST AND PRESENT

MY WIFE AND CHILDREN

AND TO MY PARENTS

IN APPRECIATION

## AUTHOR'S PREFACE

THIS book is a tale being told and covers a period of twelve years in the life of a parish. In many places the tale can only be understood if we remember that it is an account of the leading of the Holy Spirit over a period of years, and that the author is conscious both of the power of the Holy Spirit and the power of the devil in the local situation.

I would like to pay tribute to the Bishop of Ripon for his Preface to the book and also to the Bishop of Knaresborough for writing the Introduction.

Thanks are due to the late Canon J. R. Lumb, to the Rev. S. H. Evans, the Rev. A. R. Moss, the Rev. J. Elpinstone Fyffe, my colleague, the Rev. E. E. Slack, Mrs. Evelyne Holliday, and to my wife, all of whom have read the manuscript in whole or in part and have made helpful suggestions. Thanks are also due to Miss Molly Cameron for typing the whole of the manuscript, to my colleague, the Rev. J. D. Davies, for extensive help with the revision of the original manuscript, and to the Rev. Dewi Morgan for his considerable help in reducing it to the present length.

Finally, I should like to pay tribute to the people and congregation of Halton, without whose co-operation under the Holy Spirit there would have been no tale to tell.

E. W. SOUTHCOTT.

# PREFACE

By the Right Rev. GEORGE CHASE, D.D.
*Bishop of Ripon*

SOME little time ago I wrote a Foreword to a book by the Vicar of Halton with the title *Receive This Child*, in which he described the practical application of Baptismal Reform as it was being worked out in his parish. Since then this has led to considerable developments of parish policy, and these he describes in this present book.

He has throughout consulted me about what was being done, and I have had an opportunity to see it in practice and meet the people in their homes and hear from them what it has meant to them, and myself to celebrate the Holy Communion in a house-church. I think, too, that it is most important to stress the fact that, though doubtless the vicar has been the leader, he has always acted with the parish and has carefully explained to his people what he was doing and why he was doing it, and has carried them along with him, so that it is truly a parish policy.

The present is a time which calls for new and bold experiments in evangelism in our parishes. While I think it is true to say that there is not a little to give encouragement in parishes which still keep to old ways, there is a great mass of our population which is completely out of touch with the Church or with any form of Church life. Old ways leave them largely untouched. Along various lines the attempt is being made to make contact with them; for example, in the places where they work through industrial chaplains or through priest-workmen. This book tells of a different line of approach, more suitable perhaps for a parish which is not itself industrial, but which is a dormitory for people engaged in industry or business. It tells of efforts to make contact with them in the homes of the parish. But it must be emphasized that all these efforts are closely linked with the life of fellowship which finds its centre in the parish church and in the worship there, particularly in the Parish Communion. Without that close link they might well prove dangerous and divisive, rather than a building up of the one Body of Christ.

It is good that such experiments should become widely known so that Churchmen, and in particular the clergy, may get to know them, then criticize them constructively, and improve upon them. I therefore commend this account of what is being done at Halton to the consideration of those who are praying for the conversion of England. May it be used to the glory of God and the benefit of His holy Church.

✠ GEORGE RIPON.

## CONTENTS

# INTRODUCTION

By the Right Rev. Henry de Candole
*Bishop of Knaresborough*

THIS book of Canon Southcott's is a sequel to his earlier one entitled *Receive This Child*. When the child, the adult person, has been received, what then? What was he/she received into? Continue the familiar quotation: '*into the congregation*,' 'the congregation *of Christ's flock*.' That Church is, of course, the world-wide Church; indeed, the whole Church beyond the grave as well as on this side. That is why the Rite of Initiation—Baptism, Confirmation, first Communion—is once for all; the entrance door into 'the eternal kingdom which thou wast promised by Christ our Lord.' But more immediately, and visibly, it is entrance into *this* congregation, *this* local unit of the whole Church. The congregation is the outward and visible expression, *here* and *now*, of the whole Church age-long and world-wide, and beyond this life. The life of the Church is sacramental, not mainly because it possesses two, or seven, or a hundred sacraments, but because it focuses things unseen and experiences of eternity in things and experiences which can be seen and experienced visibly, tangibly, consciously. Such a sacrament the life of a Christian congregation ought to be. The baptized child or adult (and nowadays more often than formerly adults are among our newly baptized and confirmed) is received, visibly and publicly, into this congregation of Christ's flock by Baptism. But that sense of 'belonging,' of being part of a real family in Christ, should be a constant and growing experience of the newly baptized. The congregation, into which they have been received, must be a real family, or it is failing to be that 'sacrament' which it should be, a visible fact of experience rather than an elusive idea. (Does not 'the Church' too often imply an *idea* which we have to teach as part of our Confirmation instruction on the Creed rather than a *fact* of the child's daily experience?)

Canon Southcott's previous book dealt with Baptism, and touched at the end on the 'follow-up.' This book records further experiments and experiences of a congregation truly trying to be the Church, the congregation of Christ's flock in Halton. Note that all that is described below is the 'follow-up' of what was recorded earlier. These experiments are not 'stunts,' they are the exciting and adventurous attempts to map out further territory on the basis of ground already explored. Moreover, as the Preface from the diocesan bishop implies, they are made with the fullest knowledge and approval of authority, and they are based on theology. Maybe they are not for every parish—certainly not until a congregation has begun seriously to seek to live the life of 'being the Church.'

One principal discovery which is here recorded is that to be 'the Church' (the 'congregation of faithful people') is not necessarily only to be experienced in 'the church' (namely, the church building). Indeed, as may be seen, for example, in parishes which have lost their church building through the hazards of war or have not yet built one, the Church may be a true congregation, without possessing a church. Where there is a church, the Church may be experienced, and may operate, elsewhere than in the church. The Church may find herself in worship, in common prayer, in Bible study, in learning her task and her calling, in home as well as church. And, further, she may exercise her evangelistic ministry as effectively in these days, maybe even more effectively, in home than in church. This has been the experience of many recent parochial missions in which the Church has gone out from church to home, when home dwellers are too shy or unwilling to come to church. Is not this most truly to be the Church? Have we put too capital a letter on the church building, and overlaid the fact that the Church is primarily not a place but a gathering body of people—'a congregation'?

Many would agree so far. But (to mention one point which is sure to arouse discussion) the celebration of Communion in private houses—can that be justified? There is good precedent! The Eucharist was instituted in a private house—the house of the unknown host of St. Mark xiv. 14: it was celebrated by the earliest Christians in Jerusalem 'from house to house' (*Acts* ii. 46); Paul met the brethren at Troas to break bread 'in an upper chamber' (*Acts* xx. 7, 8); 'the Church in the house' of Philemon at Colosse (*Philem.* 2), of Nymphas at Laodicea (*Col.* iv. 15), of Prisca and Aquila at Rome and Ephesus (*Rom.* xvi. 5; 1 *Cor.* xvi. 19) must have shared together in the sacrament. True, when the Church grew in numbers, and was free to gather publicly, church buildings were erected, and the primary purpose of a church was a shelter for the altar, a place where the Church could gather for its supreme act of Church-manship. Was it maybe with the growing and tragic infrequency of *Communion* that more and more the church became the Mass-house, where mysteries were celebrated for, rather than shared by, the congregation? Is it perhaps because Communion has happily become again so largely throughout Christendom the normal completion of the Eucharistic celebration that we are regaining the idea of celebration in private houses? At least it is noteworthy that the 'house-church' appears in the Prayer Book; that it appears in connection with the two great sacraments of the Gospel; and that it deliberately makes provision for 'house celebrations.' 'The Ministration of Private Baptism of Children *in Houses*' is rightly regarded as exceptional, and requiring completion by the bringing of the child to 'the church' to be received 'into the congregation.' But even at private Baptism a small gathering is expected—'those that are present' are to call upon God, and say at least 'the Lord's Prayer.'

The provisions for 'the Communion of the Sick' are more detailed and more relevant. If 'the sick man be desirous to receive the Communion *in his house*, he must give timely notice to the Curate, signifying also how many there are to *communicate with* him (which shall be three, or two at the least).' If there be such 'lack of company to receive with him,' the curate is to instruct him about so-called spiritual Communion—the only exception to this insistence on a congregation being plague or such like 'contagious disease.' There in the heart of the Prayer Book is the house celebration, always implying the house-church—a representation at least of the worshipping congregation. Those who have read the diaries of seventeenth- and eighteenth-century clergymen know how faithful they were in this providing of house celebrations for the sick or dying, even when church celebrations were very infrequent. The practice of taking the Blessed Sacrament to the sick from the elements reserved in church has spread widely and happily in recent years. In many parishes (Halton included) the number of sick communicants could not be otherwise served, and Communion from the altar in church has its own message of union with the worshipping family. But it can easily become purely individual ministration, a receiving (indeed) of the sacred elements, but scarcely a 'Com-munion,' and perhaps we should—as so often—take the Prayer Book more fully at its word, and be more ready to celebrate in houses and thus restore the Church in the house. The writer will not soon forget such a celebration on Maundy Thursday afternoon at the kitchen table of a cottage in a Sussex hamlet: the table spread with a white tablecloth, the old husband and wife sitting round, and after they had received Communion the elements being taken up to the dying shepherd, her brother, in his bed upstairs. There are many not only in bodily sickness, yet aged and infirm, hindered by family and other duties, or far from church, to whom such a coming of the Church to their house, a gathering of neighbours, would mean perhaps the real possibility of sharing in the Church's corporate worship from which circumstances had prevented them. This surely is one practical method of ministration in the distant farm-houses and hamlets of our large country parishes and groups of parishes—nor are such hindered people to be found only in the country. By meeting practical necessities in this way others, clergy and laity alike, might come to learn what Halton has learned thereby, both of the theology of the Church, and of the practical experience of 'being the Church' which it brings.

There are those who may feel more doubtful of the celebration of the Eucharist in the presence of the lapsed or unconfirmed. But if the Church is the Body of Christ, then the congregation of the faithful is bringing Him to these wandering sheep and the evangelistic power of the Breaking of the Bread is vividly described in these pages. Moreover, these are, as Canon Southcott stresses, not the heathen but the lapsed *baptized*—members, if 'careless' ones, of the family. We do not close the doors of our churches at the celebration of the Eucharist to all but faithful members. Many a parish priest will celebrate the Eucharist for his school children, baptized or unbaptized and mostly unconfirmed. May there not be a converting power in the Lord's presence at the worship of the faithful to draw back the careless? Experience has found there is. Certainly the writer would testify to the privilege and encouragement of being present recently at a series of house celebrations, night and morning, in preparation for the annual Confirmation, and to the joy of confirming in their own houses, but in the presence of groups of the faithful, a number of ill or house-fast candidates—in two cases, elderly couples together—and of giving them their first Communion there and then.

There is always the suggestion that new and adventurous methods of church life and witness are 'newfangled' and therefore self-condemned. They may indeed upset ways that have been conventional and therefore accepted as right and normal. But it is at least pertinent to ask which are more consonant both with the Prayer Book pattern and the sound (though often neglected) theology of worship on which it is based—the ways which have become accepted, *or* the ways which are being discovered, experimented with, or (more truly) rediscovered? Baptism in an almost empty church, *or* 'when the most number of people come together'? The Communion divorced from the ministry of the Word, *or* with the sermon which 'shall follow' the Creed? A sick communion with no other to communicate, *or* with 'three, or two at the least'? The children of the congregation segregated into special groups, *or* worshipping with, 'hearing sermons' with, and taught in the presence of their elders? The newly confirmed without *or* with 'Godfather or Godmother' behind to support them? Sinners (that is, all men) made aware of the provision, if they need it, of 'the benefit of absolution' through 'a minister of God's Word,' *or* allowed to live in ignorance of it? Dying persons taught how to prepare for death, *or* left without the instruction and the strength provided by the Church for her children? It is among other things to such reassessment of our practice in living the life of 'the congregation of Christ's flock' that this book and the experiences recorded in it recall us. By such a conviction of mission THE PARISH COMES ALIVE.

✠ HENRY KNARESBOROUGH.

# THE PARISH COMES ALIVE

## CHAPTER I

## *THE REVOLUTIONARY COMMUNITY*

THE Abbé Michonneau autographed my copy of *Revolution in a City Parish*, 'From the community of St. Pierre and St. Paul to the Community of St. Wilfrid, Halton.' He disapproved of the English title given to his book, and he would have preferred *The Parish—A Revolutionary Community*. There, in brief, is the vocation of the Christian congregation. When the parish is a community in which God is discovered and rediscovered, in which Christ is shown forth, in which the Holy Spirit is experienced, it is revolutionary and dynamic. It is a community in which people see more and more of the love of God and do more and more about it. Maritain has said that every age has its relative pattern of holiness and the relative pattern of holiness for to-day is community. The Church is *the* community.

The Church throughout the world and the local church are called to live out this life of community. In the Church and through the Church the common life in the Body of Christ is to be experienced in the world. The Church is to bring to the world the fullness, the wholeness, of Christ. Paul 'looks upon Christ as in a sense waiting for completeness, and destined in the purpose of God to find completeness in the Church.'[1]

The Church is to bring the fullness, the wholeness, of Christ in three respects. First it is to bring it to the whole of creation. Life is a whole, creation is a unity, not in itself, but in God. We see this most characteristically when Christ meets His Church in the Holy Communion.

[1] Armitage Robinson, *St. Paul's Epistle to the Ephesians*, p. 42.

The whole of creation is with the priest and the congregation at the Lord's table. All created things are offered there; all created things are incomplete without Christ; and every created thing is to be used as reverently as the bread and wine is used in the Communion.

The Church is also to bring the wholeness of Christ to the whole of mankind. It is for every one or for no one. The Church which is His Body is to go into all the world, not just part of it; to make disciples of all nations, not just some of them—baptizing all of them and teaching all of them and remembering the Lord is with them, even unto the end of the world. In this way, all men are to become *whole*. To the scientist; to the economist; to the politician; to the engineer; to the farmer; to the housewife, the Church is to bring the wholeness of Christ. All mankind stands with the priest at the Lord's Table.

And the Church is to bring the completeness, the wholeness of Christ to the whole man. Each person as a member of the community is 'to grow unto the measure of the stature of the fullness of Christ.' Sin and disease prevent Christ's wholeness. So the Church is to minister to the sick in mind, body, and spirit, and thus in a wonderful way to complete Christ. Thus the Church is a redeemed and a redeeming community, carrying on Christ's atoning work for the whole of creation. There is a Zulu saying, 'If there is a thorn in the foot, the whole body must stoop down and take it out.' Wherever there is incompleteness, disease, ill health, mistrust, misunderstanding, untruth, there at that point the Church is called to bring Christ's wholeness, His fullness.

There is a movement throughout Christendom, a movement of the Holy Spirit in His Church, to bring this wholeness, this fullness to the world. It is a proclamation of the Gospel in terms of fellowship. The Zoe movement in Greece, the Iona movement in Scotland, the liturgical movement in France, Parish-field in America, the Kirchentag in Germany, the Parish and People Movement in this country, are among its manifestations.

Ultimately, the evidence for the credibility of the Gospel in the eyes of the world will rest upon the evidence of a quality of life manifested in the Church which the world cannot find elsewhere.

The report *Towards the Conversion of England* stresses that the acid test of Christianity is the fellowship in the Church. Dr. McLeod, in *We Shall Re-build*, states:

> His plan is not that a number of separate persons must become united with Him and in mutual isolation be His instruments for the redemption of the world. His instrument is a fellowship, His continuing mystical Body on earth, in which we are members incorporate. It is this outgoing and outgiving organism that He has created for the saving of the world. Constant and corporate mission belongs, therefore, to the essence of the Church's life.

The Abbé Michonneau, in *Revolution in a City Parish*, insists:

> Let each parish strive to make its liturgy splendid and full of meaning. Let each parish make of itself a real community, devoted to the conquest of souls, and united within itself for that single goal.

Lord (Eustace) Percy, in *The Christian Congregation*, states:

> The purpose of God is to 'gather into one all things in Christ,' and the centre of that purpose is the Body of Christ. . . . I have tried to suggest at least one answer to the question of what healing Christians have to bring to this half-destroyed world. This answer . . . is the revival of the Christian congregation.

At the end of a diocesan conference I was addressing in December, 1949, the Bishop of Bradford sent his clergy and lay people back to their parishes to ask their congregations two questions: (1) 'Are we the Body of Christ, or just a group of people who go to church?' (2) 'Have we a parish policy?' As members of the Body of Christ, we are called into a holy community, a community constantly being called out of the world and constantly being sent back into the world. The Church is most characteristically itself when its members are being baptized, breaking bread, bearing witness.

'Where can I meet the Church? Where can I meet the Church in action?' 'Come and see; yes, come and see a Baptism.' Would the administration of the great evangelical sacrament of Baptism be a great common act of worship proclaiming the Gospel?

'Where can I meet the Church?' 'Come and see; yes, come to the breaking of bread.' Would it be a great act of common worship; would all ages be represented; would the preaching of the word be an integral part; would the offertory stress creation's part in it and would there be a general Communion?

'Where can I meet the Church? Where can I meet the Church in action?' 'Come and see; yes, come to the Parochial Church Council, the Mothers' Union, the youth club, the whist drive, the social, the dance.'

'But do I meet the *Church* there?' 'No, only a bit of it. You must come to the parish meeting.'

The Church is not fully the Church unless it gathers together all ages and sexes to wait upon the Spirit, to discuss what it means to be a Christian congregation, to be a mission station, to actualize what is sacramentally given in Communion, to work out a common parish policy. The Lambeth Conference reminded us that the local congregation is the place where men must find the life of the great Church which is God's instrument for the world's salvation; and the Malvern Conference reminded us that 'the whole congregation habitually worshipping together should meet regularly.' The annual meeting, special parochial church meetings, the Parochial Church Council, the electoral roll, and the various sectional meetings—all can help; but in each parish a regular meeting of the congregation is also needed to build fellowship within the congregation and between the congregation and the society around it.

In Halton it was this meeting of the congregation, the parish meeting, that helped the Church to be more fully the Church when it baptizes, breaks bread, bears witness. From the parish meeting the Church has been gradually driven out into the parish, into the homes of the people. We have also been driven outside the parish into fellowship with other parishes inside and outside the diocese. In all we do we are in touch with our diocesan, the Bishop of Ripon, and he has given his full approval at every stage. We are striving to be true to our Anglican tradition and we are discovering what it means to *be* the Church in the house, in the parish, in the diocese, in the world.

## NOTE

The Chairman of the Parish and People Movement in Great Britain is the Bishop of Knaresborough, and the Secretary is the Rev. Kenneth Packard, Lower Heyford Rectory, Oxford.

## CHAPTER II

## *LET THE CHURCH EXULT*

HAVE we a parish policy about admitting new members into the family of God, we asked ourselves. We wouldn't take a baby after it was born and say, 'Now you're born, get on with it!' It would soon die. A child has to be placed in the best possible environment to grow up a healthy member of the Smith family and of the human race.

So, a child when admitted to the family of God as an infant needs to be surrounded with care and attention by the local congregation, parents and godparents. Canon J. R. Lumb has described baptismal registers as the story of the Church's forgotten children. We have a National Society for the Prevention of Cruelty to Children. The Church's neglect of her children is something that needs just as much attention. We wouldn't dream of separating a child at birth from home and parents, and yet ninety per cent of the children brought to our fonts are brought with no real intention of building them up in the Christian family, and bringing them regularly to the heavenly Father's house to receive nourishment and help.

At a Parochial Church Council meeting at Halton on Parish Evangelism one of the members asked, 'What about Joe Bloggs? What has all this emphasis on Baptism to do with him?' Joe Bloggs is one of the great mass of baptized incorporated into the fellowship of the Church. He is an engineer with a real sense of responsibility to home and work, but no sense of the relevance of the Church, except for 'Hatches, Matches, and Dispatches.' How is he to be helped from where he is to where he ought to be—a vital member of the worshipping community?

Should we make Baptism difficult to have and therefore more respected?

The Lambeth Report wisely states: 'A hasty adoption of any policy of widespread exclusion from Baptism would be wrong.' How is Joe Bloggs to be helped to see that Baptism is what Fr. Benson of Cowley called 'The Greater Sacrament'? Canon Roger Lloyd says:

> The real trouble is that the spirit of Baptism in the early Church no longer applies, where, after initiation, there followed the Easter Mass in the dawn and first Communion as the beginning of the Christian life in the midst of the exultant Church.[1]

Exultant is the ringing word in that sentence. We have made it almost impossible for members of the Church to *exult* because a new member of the Church has been admitted. 'Let the Church exult.' Let the Church be the Church, then Christian initiation will be seen in all its fullness.[2]

In passing, be it noted that it is almost impossible for members of the Church fully to exult at the admission of new members while the Church is divided, while it seems to be as important to claim to be Methodist or Baptist or Anglican as to be Christian, while the Church appears to be a series of competitive clubs.

In the pre-Nicene Church, renunciation, confession of faith, anointing with oil, imposition of hands, and first Communion were frequently called 'a Baptism.' Further, Baptism was a public act of worship at certain seasons of the year, such as Easter Eve and Whitsun, and the local congregation was there, the local embodiment of the world-wide and ageless Church.

Here is the fullness of Christian initiation and it is reflected in the Book of Common Prayer, which presupposes a teaching and worshipping community in which Baptism, catechizing, Confirmation, Communion,

[1] Roger Lloyd, *The Church of England in the Twentieth Century*, Vol. 2, p. 61, quoting Dix, *The Theology of Confirmation in Relation to Baptism*.

[2] A fuller exposition of this will be found in my book *Receive This Child*, published by A. R. Mowbray & Co. Limited, 3s.

may be separated in time but never in intention. It also presupposes Baptism in the presence of the congregation at a liturgical service, for it is one of the common acts of the people of God.

As congregations become more alive to the meaning of Christian initiation, godparents will more and more be chosen from regular worshippers: Canon 31 is very clear that godparents must be confirmed. But if the Church, and in particular the ministry of the Church, has allowed this to lapse, we must exercise a real charity towards those who bring their children to church for Baptism, but who have never been themselves fully incorporated into the Body of Christ.

As Joe Bloggs sees the meaning of the Church and the fullness of Christian initiation, he and his wife will ask responsible Churchmen to answer on behalf of their child. And as Baptism becomes less and less another domestic occasion and becomes more and more an ecclesiastical one, people will begin to refuse to take promises they don't understand or are unable to keep themselves.

As the Church faces the implications of this it may well lead to one communicant sponsor and both parents answering for the child as is recommended by the Lambeth Report, for the real responsibility of bringing the child up in the worshipping community is with the parents.

This has led to encouraging both parents to return thanks—it has led to personal interviews in the home before and after the Baptism—it has led to less frequent Baptism services, to giving more time for preparation. It has led to a meeting of the parents and godparents with the congregation before the Baptism, preceded by a rehearsal. It has led to 'banns' of Baptism being read out in the face of the congregation on the previous Sunday. It has led to a gathering in the hall after the Baptism for the presenting of Baptism cards to parents and godparents. It has led to home meetings and house celebrations of the Holy Communion to follow up the Baptism and personal visits with Baptism anniversary cards.

Often the Church has administered the sacrament of Baptism without preaching the Word—a reason for much of the inadequate understanding of Christian membership. But even when the Word has been preached, before, during, and after the service, and even when the Word of God has been received gladly, the majority of parents are miles away from the worshipping community. Joe Bloggs often has a sense of integrity in his home and work, which applied to Church membership would be good for Joe and good for the Church. The fathers present at one public Baptism in Halton included an engineer, a baker, a solicitor's clerk; and there were many others. There it seems to me is the focal point to-day for the Church's task of evangelism. Help these people to see that the most important thing about them is not that they are engineers, bakers, clerks, but that they are *baptized* engineers, *baptized* bakers, *baptized* clerks.

This is the task of the local congregation, not just of the parson. The excellent report from the Church of England Children's Council, *Children Adrift*, has a pamphlet based on it entitled *Action Stations*, which begins: 'All baptized children are the responsibility of the whole congregation.' This has led in Halton to the congregation attending the service and joining with the priest in saying, 'We receive this child into the congregation of Christ's flock. . . .' It has led to Confirmation candidates being expected to attend Baptism services as well as Parish Communion as part of their preparation for Confirmation; the two evangelical sacraments are regarded as normal parts of their public worship. It has led to Sunday school and children's work being regarded as a sort of catechumenate, leading up to Confirmation and regular Communion. It has led to the moving of the font from a side chapel into the centre of the building; it has led to Church people offering to be sponsors when communicants cannot be found by the parents. It has led to sponsors for Confirmation candidates who really do stand behind the young communicants, inside and outside the church building. It has led to meetings of the Parochial Church Council and the congregation, to work out the parish policy about their common responsibility for the baptized. It has led to conventions, missions, and home meeting weeks, to help to make membership more effective. It has led members of Church organizations, Sunday school teachers, and others to become more aware of their responsibilities towards the newly baptized and their parents.

The local congregation must assume its responsibilities for the new members of the Church and thus will the fullness of the Gospel be more and more proclaimed to the world. In the total immersion in water, which is symbolized in Baptism, the Church proclaims the totality of God's claim on the whole of man's life. No longer can Baptism be divorced from Confirmation, from worship, from conversion—St. Augustine said, 'Infants are baptized in order that they may be converted'; no longer can Baptism be divorced from Christian vocation in the world.

CHAPTER III

# THE PATTERN OF SUNDAY WORSHIP

IN 1949 the Archbishops of Canterbury and York issued a form of service to commemorate the 400th anniversary of the Book of Common Prayer. It took the following form: Mattins beginning with 'O Lord, open Thou our lips,' with the *Benedictus* as an introit, then the Litany, followed immediately by the Communion service. This was to be one service, as had been the original intention for morning worship, and was to be followed in the afternoon or evening by Evensong. It was obviously the intention that Sunday worship should be, so to speak, a three-course meal—first course, Mattins; second course, Communion; third course, Evensong. In the Church of England to-day some people have made the first course the main part of the meal, some the third course, while others have said, 'Communion is all that matters.' One of the things that puzzles people in the parish churches up and down the country is why there is this variety of services, when it is obvious in the New Testament and the early Church that the Lord's day became the Lord's day because the Eucharist was held on the first day of the week to celebrate Christ's Resurrection.

Let us look back at the Middle Ages: the layman became, as he is so often now, a mere spectator.

It we put all these things, the isolation of the priesthood of the priest from the corporate offering; the false theory of a separate value of the sacrifice of the Mass from the sacrifice of Calvary; the elimination of the layman's 'liturgy' of offering and Communion, which makes the Holy Communion (in practice) a part of the celebrant's liturgy and nobody else's; the reduction of the laity's part in the rite to 'seeing' and 'hearing' (the latter being reduced very much in importance through the use of Latin, which placed an over-emphasis on 'seeing' the consecrated sacrament), and in consequence of all these, the placing of the whole devotional emphasis in the rite on the consecration and conversion of the elements—if we put all these things together, we can see what the medieval liturgical development is doing. It is steadily building up the material for all the doctrinal controversies about the Eucharist in the sixteenth century. And I believe that it can be shown that in all their mistakes the Reformers were the victims—as they were the products—of the medieval deformations they opposed.[1]

In the Middle Ages most people attended Mass, but relatively few received Communion. The Reformers unfortunately tried to compel people to communicate more frequently by the threat of depriving them of the Mass if they didn't. One of the rubrics from the end of the Communion service says—'And there shall be no celebration of the Lord's Supper, except there be a convenient number to communicate with the priest, according to his discretion (which shall be three, or two at least).' So comes the development of Ante-Communion, and the usual Sunday programme in the late sixteenth century came to be 6 a.m. Mattins, 8 a.m. Litany and Ante-Communion. Later, of course, Mattins was deferred and joined with Litany and Ante-Communion and the whole service postponed to a convenient hour after breakfast. So, in some Prayer Books printed in the eighteenth century the part of the Holy Communion service after the Prayer for the Church was in very small type, presumably because it was so seldom used.

This arrangement of the service was that found by the Evangelicals, who revived the weekly Communion, and the Tractarians, who specially wanted it every Sunday at an hour when people could communicate fasting. So came the 8 a.m. plain celebration which is still found in most of our churches. The Tractarians developed the solemn celebration of Holy Communion at a later hour,

[1] Dom Gregory Dix, *The Shape of the Liturgy*, p. 598.

preceded in some cases by said Mattins. In some churches Mattins alone was retained and the connection with the Communion forgotten, and this has become for many the ordinary morning service; in others, again, there was Mattins and Ante-Communion for the greater part of the congregation and Communion for the few. This is the situation which the Liturgical Movement has tried to meet.

There is no shadow of doubt that the Liturgical Movement is backed up by biblical theology. The people of God are to meet for the breaking of the bread on the first day of the week as the most characteristic action of the Body of Christ. The Prayer Book certainly means the main service on Sunday to be the Communion service with sermon, notices, and so on. But it is quite obvious, too, that in 1549 the Anglican Church drew up a pattern of daily common worship; Mattins and Evensong were to be said daily with the Book of Psalms divided into portions for each morning and evening, and with lessons to cover roughly the reading of the Old Testament once and the New Testament twice during each year. Not until 1922 did the Church recognize that this had broken down and provide special lessons for Sundays.

The 400th anniversary of the English Prayer Book gave us at Halton an opportunity of facing up to the challenge of the three-course diet. Up to that time Mattins had no real place in the worship of the general congregation, and a generation of young people was growing up without hearing the Old Testament, the Psalms, and the *Te Deum* and *Benedictus*. On June 19, 1949, we followed the authorized *Order of Divine Service*. Subsequently, after considerable discussion with the Parochial Church Council and congregation and with the permission of the diocesan bishop, for an experimental period of three months we had an introduction to the Communion service which took the following form: 'O Lord, open Thou our lips' to the end of the psalms for the day, as in Mattins for the Sunday; an

Old Testament lesson based on the gospel for the day; on alternate Sundays the *Te Deum* or the *Benedictus* as the introit to the Communion service. Whatever else this was, it was not Mattins; so for the next three years we sang Mattins before the Parish Communion, beginning with 'O Lord, open Thou our lips,' saying the psalms for the Sunday and using Table A, Table B, or the 1922 Tables of Lessons, and singing both canticles with the *Benedictus* as the introit to the Communion. We found that with episcopally authorized lay help in the administration of the chalice the services together never took more than ten minutes longer than the Parish Communion alone.

Since our campaign (then called a mission) in October, 1952, we have become growingly convinced that we ought to be helping people to come step by step right into the centre of the worshipping community, the central act of which is the Eucharist. One of the questions we have been asking ourselves is, 'Where do the Sunday offices fit into the general aim and policy?' At the time of the mission we saw the need for a form of service in the parish church on Sunday to which non-worshippers could come; so on Sunday evening we used a service of hymns, Bible readings, sermon, and all the parts of prayer, carefully based on a definite theme for each service. These theme services or people's services did help some people to come into the worshipping fellowship and we learned by practice different ways of prayer, but relatively few were drawn in permanently. From this experience we tried to see what the future programme ought to be. This was expressed at the annual meeting, 1953, as follows:

In 1953 in Halton we recognize that there is a need for a service on Sunday other than Mattins, Communion, or Evensong, which will help people to worship God in their parish church. We recognize the fact that we cannot run two evening services, and also that Evensong is neither supported by the majority of the morning congregation, nor meant to be a popular service. Further, Mattins and Evensong belong together and we want the mind of the congregation on whether it is best to carry on with the Sunday programme as in Lent or not. Mattins and Evensong could be sung, for instance, in Advent and Lent at 9 a.m. and 6 p.m. respectively so that people have the opportunity of occasionally taking part in the fuller worship of the Book of Common Prayer.

We have discussed this further at P.C.C. and parish meetings and home meetings, and it is still too early to decide what the pattern of Sunday worship is to be here. There are obviously some who think that sung Mattins and Parish Communion and Evensong should be the pattern (the arrangement of the Church's lessons and psalms intends the people of God to hear both morning and evening prayer on Sunday); others prefer said Mattins at 9 a.m., Parish Communion at 9.30 a.m.: while others are prepared to accept Parish Communion and some sort of people's service in the evening as the future pattern, with Mattins and Evensong said on Sundays as it is on weekdays. What we are attempting to do is to think out and pray out what our Sunday worship ought to be. Up until Advent, 1954, it included all three of the above patterns at different times of the year.

During this whole period we had been feeling after some integration of Mattins and Parish Communion; on Septuagesima Sunday, 1955, we used the following form of service:

'O Lord, open Thou our lips,' and its responses, sung at the vestry door.
*Venite* sung in procession to the sanctuary.
Psalms as appointed for Mattins.
Our Father: Collect for Purity, said together.
Ninefold 'Have mercy.'
Collect for the Queen.
Collect(s) for the day.
Old Testament lesson as appointed for Mattins, read by a layman from the lectern.

*Te Deum.*

Epistle, as announced, read by a lay reader from the pulpit.

*Benedictus.*

Gospel, as announced, read by one of the clergy.

Creed, sermon, hymn, offertory, biddings, Prayer for the Church, and the rest of the service as described in the next chapter.

This was accepted by the annual meeting in April, 1955, and after a year it has proved to be the form of morning worship that best stresses the word and sacrament together. We have been encouraged in this by the *Minneapolis Report.*[1] The Bible is now brought in at the beginning of the service by the celebrant and placed on a prayer desk near the chancel step, and is kept there open throughout the week. The readers of the Old Testament lesson, the epistle and gospel, and the preacher take it from the desk to the lectern and pulpit. For this use of the Bible to be really effective the Church will have to revise its lectionary so as to provide Old Testament lessons that fit the epistle and gospels, for it is in the liturgy that first and foremost the people of God are to learn to understand the Scriptures.[2]

We are keeping before us the two main aims of our worship on Sunday—to help us all to make as worthy an offering to God as we can and to help those who do not habitually worship in their parish church to do so.

If Mattins and Evensong are both offices of the initiated rather than the uninitiated, it is very doubtful whether they ought ever to be pushed on the outsider. It may be that Parish Communion and people's service is to become the normal and that the people's service will become more and more what the French liturgiologists would call para-liturgy. It may still be right at

[1] Report of the Editorial Committee, p. 198. The Dean of Lincoln, p. 98.

[2] This is provided in the liturgy of the Church of South India.

certain seasons of the year like Advent and Lent to have sung Mattins before Parish Communion, and Evensong before people's service, to give the regular worshipper an opportunity to have a fuller expression of the liturgy of morning and evening prayer. On the other hand, it may be true that the majority of the lapsed baptized are so far removed from the worshipping community that it will be some time yet before they are ready even for a people's service, or at least a people's service in the parish church. So on the first two Sundays in Advent, 1953, instead of having sung Evensong at 6 p.m. followed immediately by people's service in church, we sang Evensong at 6 p.m. and moved out for 7.30 p.m. to five houses, and in each of these houses a short evening service was held, conducted by lay people. This may well become a normal feature of our Sunday programme; but if it does we shall need to watch for opportunities of building the people of these homes into the worshipping community. It may be that we shall build them into Parish Communion, it may be that we shall build them into Evensong, or it may be that we shall build them into some form of people's service in the parish church.

The important thing is that we should be alert to our responsibility towards the parish as a whole. We began having these house services in the homes of sick or elderly people or other folk who for some reason or other cannot come to the church building: these people have welcomed the opportunity of having services in their houses, so we are discovering the Church outside the church building. In 1954 we planned that ten of these house services should take place after Evensong every first Sunday in the month, still in the houses of worshipping Christians who cannot get to church. They were all conducted by lay people, sometimes all by young people. Recently another parish in Leeds was holding a mission in which we assisted in various ways, and on the Sunday before it started we used their broadcast service for our house services. So we shared in it by having congregations taking part in it in homes up and down the parish. It is quite clear that these house services have met a real need in this parish. We are so convinced about this that from September, 1956, we are planning to decentralize Evensong itself, having ten house Evensongs every Sunday and having Evensong simply said in church, with hymns. Regular teams of people will take these Evensongs, and the whole wealth of the liturgy of the Word will be available for those people who are mature in the faith but who are unable to get to the church building. All this seems to be a quite natural development of being the Church—the Church inside and outside the church building, inside and outside the parish.

## CHAPTER IV

# *LET THE LITURGY BE SPLENDID*

WE see the Church most characteristically herself when she meets to break bread. Members of the Church are never more their true selves than at the Communion service; this is the most manly thing any one can do. Here we offer and present ourselves, our souls and bodies, to be a reasonable, holy, and lively sacrifice. *The Shape of the Liturgy* by Dom Gregory Dix could be summed up in the sentence, 'The Eucharist is an action, an action of Christ in the Church.' Is it true that people coming to this service would *see* the Church in action?

Nowhere at the moment is the liturgy the action of the *whole* people of God, nowhere is there a true *Parish* Communion: while the Church is divided the liturgy cannot be a completely splendid offering to God or a completely meaningful proclamation to the world.

Is it true that the congregation realize that the Communion is the Church in action? Often we regard the service as something done by some one else—the celebrant, the servers, and so on.

Our Member of Parliament was very moved by the Coronation service, but in his description of it he commented that the weakness was the congregation! One felt that this was typical of the Church of England. The queen, the archbishop, the other bishops and officiants, the choir and so forth, did their part well; three per cent of the congregation did their part well, but the ninety-seven per cent didn't!

A priest was once taking an early celebration, during the course of which he discovered there were seven or eight people present who were all behind different pillars! These people were, no doubt, very devoted and received great help from their Communion and, perhaps, at real inconvenience to themselves had come out early on a Sunday morning, but the congregation as it expressed itself was not fully the Church in action. Such an attitude does not help the communicants to see their corporate responsibility for mission. If it is true that members of the Church are never more their true selves than at the Communion service, then it is a tragedy that while seventy per cent of the babies born in 1954 were baptized at the fonts of the Church of England, less than one per cent will, at the present rate, become regular weekly communicants. I believe that we are meant to be trained in the liturgy in order that we may take corporate action outside the Communion service. This is one of the ways in which we are to let the liturgy be splendid.

We must help people to take part in the liturgy, to realize that it is their liturgy and that this is the people of God acting together. Dom Gregory Dix makes a point that the general Communion went out of the liturgy at the same time as the emphasis on the offertory was neglected. In the early Church, the Sunday Eucharist was often like a miniature harvest festival. From the offerings in kind the offertory of bread and wine was taken and what was left was distributed to those who were in need. But when this died out the layman became, as he is so often now, 'a mere spectator and listener, without a "liturgy" in the primitive sense at all.' The right doctrine of creation as well as the right doctrine of recreation is stressed in the offertory. The separation of Christ from His creation is brought home when people say, 'Ordinary bread is not good enough for Communion.' We are not now entering into a controversy about leavened or unleavened bread; both have Catholic support —the Eastern Church uses leavened bread and the Western Church uses unleavened bread. At Halton for three years we used each on alternate Sundays. Now we use alternately bought bread and home-made bread given by members of the congregation. Whatever other arguments may be used for wafer bread, certainly that of convenience is very strong; but if we are not offering the whole of fallen creation in penitence to God in the offertory we miss something of the meaning of redemption and something of the meaning of the Communion service.

This separation of Christ from creation is a fundamental heresy which has very serious consequences. If we once divorce Christ from any part of life this is heresy. In the Communion service our Lord takes the ordinary food and drink of the day, as a means whereby He comes anew to recreate and redeem and renew. Whether we use leavened or unleavened bread is quite secondary as long as we lay claim to the whole of creation when we celebrate Holy Communion. Indeed, it is true that the whole of creation stands with the priest and congregation.

It is a most wonderful thing that the second Person of the Holy Trinity should take our flesh, and it is just as wonderful that He should take bread and wine, man's ordinary daily food, and give Himself to us in them. The divine purpose underlying the two acts is the same, the sacrament flows from the Incarnation. The Word became flesh in order to redeem the whole man. Similarly, our Lord takes to Himself bread and wine that He may become the food of the whole man. He might have communicated Himself to our souls apart from material means, but then He would not have been the food of our whole being. He came to save people, not souls only.

There can be no false separation between liturgy and society—between the sacred and the secular—for the Church of the Incarnate Lord. The Communion service is meant to be a means of Christ's reclaiming of the whole of life. The Church is apostolic inasmuch as it is sent forth to claim every part of life for Christ.

For this reason the offertory in the Holy Communion service has a special importance, for at this point representative elements are taken from the 'secular' context and are made ready for the 'sacred.' It therefore needs a special emphasis. The meaning of offertory is brought out by each person placing a piece of bread in the ciborium as he comes into the church. Each piece of bread offered represents our life and work offered to God, the imperfect life, the imperfect work. After the ministry of the Word in the sermon, in Halton the crucifer and candle-bearers pass down through the congregation to the west end and the procession forms up as follows:

> Cross and candles, sidesmen with the alms, two representatives of the congregation (male and female, younger and older) with the cruets, the churchwardens with the ciborium and second chalice, the reader with the first chalice.

The whole procession moves up through the congregation and at the Communion rail the alms are received and placed on the altar, the ciborium is placed on the altar, the celebrant prepares the chalices facing the people during an interval in the hymn; when the alms and oblations are all placed on the altar the celebrant turns to the people saying, 'The Lord be with you,' and the congregation responds, 'And with thy spirit.' Priest and people then say together the offertory sentence, 'All things come of Thee, O Lord, and of Thine own have we given Thee.' Thus the Church's offering is underlined and the Church acts together in the offertory.

The special biddings which come at this point are taken from the body of the church; they include a missionary intention for the week, a diocese and bishop for the day, our own diocese and bishops, a parish intention for the day, the sick and departed by name, and any personal prayers or thanksgivings that are desired. These are summed up in the Prayer for the Church Militant, read from the middle of the nave, read, like the epistle, by a layman.

One thing we do not offer is an impenitent heart, and the offertory is incomplete without personal preparation on the part of each member of the congregation. One of the dangers of Parish Communion is that people will come without preparation. The two exhortations in the Prayer Book, following the Prayer for the Church, are very wise. The first reminds us of the great danger we are in by coming unprepared; the second reminds us of the danger if we don't come at all. The first exhortation states:

> And because it is requisite, that no man should come to the Holy Communion, but with a full trust in God's mercy, and with a quiet conscience; therefore if there be any of you, who by this means cannot quiet his own conscience herein, but requireth further comfort or counsel, let him come to me, or to some other discreet and learned minister of God's Word, and open his grief; that by the ministry of God's holy Word he may receive the benefit of absolution, together with ghostly counsel and advice, to the quieting of his conscience, and avoiding of all scruple and doubtfulness.

The second exhortation states:

> So it is your duty to receive the Communion in remembrance of the sacrifice of His death, as He Himself hath commanded: which if ye shall neglect to do, consider with yourselves how great injury ye do unto God, and how sore punishment hangeth over your heads for the same; when ye wilfully abstain from the Lord's Table, and separate from your brethren, who come to feed on the banquet of that most heavenly food.

In the Communion service there follows the invitation to the confession, 'Ye that do truly and earnestly repent'—(look in)—'And are in love and charity with your neighbours'—(look round)—'And intend to lead a new life following the commandments of God'—(look forward)—'Draw near with faith'—(look up).

It seems right to stand for the *Sursum Corda* as it seems right to kneel for the confession. God has given us bodies and I believe He means us to use them when we worship. God does come in a wonderful way to enrich our lives however the Communion is celebrated, whether as a quiet said service without a sermon, or high Mass without Communion: but surely the fullness of it is brought out if the offertory, the consecration, the Communion, are all seen as the Church acting together. This Church stretches right round the world, and beyond this world to where by far the greater number of our members are: so we say, 'Holy, holy, holy, Lord God of hosts, heaven and earth are full of Thy glory.' We then drop on our knees for the Prayer of Humble Access. In Halton we always say it together as, incidentally, the revised Canadian Prayer Book recommends. We find value in saying the Collect for Purity together too.

For the Prayer of Consecration it has been customary to kneel and certainly the custom is a good one; it suggests an attitude of reverence and devotion and expectancy. The alternative is to stand, together, shoulder to shoulder round the altar, to stress the truth that the priest is celebrating in the Name of Christ and on behalf of the people of God. This would certainly make it more possible for the amen at the end of the prayer to ring out like a thunder clap—as St. Jerome suggested it did. With modern pews and chairs it is next to impossible to stand together, shoulder to shoulder, so it is best to kneel but to join fully in the amen as the most important amen in the service.

When Dr. Nicholas Zernov, the Eastern Orthodox theologian, came to our Parish Communion he heard the Prayer of Oblation said by the whole congregation after the pause following the Prayer of Consecration. He said he rejoiced when he heard it, and always felt that the Prayer of Oblation simply shouted to be said together. In this way it becomes the very wonderful response to what God so wonderfully does for us in this Holy Sacrifice. And this we realize most individually and personally in the general Communion; yet here above all we are most together, for here, openly and sacramentally, we, God and His people, make *our*

Communion in the only valid sense of that phrase. This is summed up in the Lord's Prayer, for it is then alone we dare say *our* Father, and the service finishes with the Prayer of Thanksgiving, *Gloria*, and Blessing.

Instead of the usual vestry prayers we have a corporate congregational prayer with the choir and servers; we say together a prayer such as that of St. Ignatius, St. Richard of Chichester, St. Francis, or a suitable collect. This prayer is followed by: 'The Lord be with you. And with thy spirit. Let us bless the Lord. Thanks be to God. Let us go forth in peace. In the Name of Christ, Amen.' This brings out the same meaning as the *Ite Missa Est* of the Roman rite of Holy Communion.

The meaning of the *Ite Missa Est* is carried a step further in the parish breakfast which follows. The importance of this is specially brought out when it is held after the first Communion of the newly confirmed.

Until 1955 on the Sunday before the Confirmation week-end the chairs in the whole of the front of the church were moved to the side and four rows were placed against the chancel step facing west. A nave altar was placed near the font, right in the midst of the congregation. The Communion rails were placed completely round the altar and the priest celebrated in the midst of the people, facing west. This arrangement is particularly helpful to the Confirmation candidates, and both the candidates and the regular members of the congregation have said how much they have learned from it. For three years this has been the arrangement of the church for weekdays and in 1955 we have started to use it for the Parish Communion on Sundays in Advent and Lent also. For a three-month period we celebrated facing the people from the high altar, but decided that although it was right to celebrate facing the people at the nave altar, it was right to celebrate facing east at the high altar.

The symbolism of the Eastern Orthodox Church with its complete screen and the sacred ministers celebrating behind it, stresses most strongly the Communion of Saints; heaven is just beyond the screen and the liturgy brings heaven down to earth. The Orthodox Church aims to bring heaven down to earth, and the Western Church aims to lift earth up to heaven—and both are right. Would not they both be realized by the altar in the centre of the church?

I have wondered about the possibility of building a church with the ground plan of the Maltese cross. We would enter such a church in the middle and immediately encounter an altar with a circular Communion rail and a font. Immediately we would see the connection between the home and the parish church: altar and table, font and wash-basin. All people need to eat and wash. In the home and in the parish church alike we need feeding and cleansing. In the word and in the sacrament Christ comes to cleanse and to feed. In my new church building there would be a painting in the dome of Christ reigning in glory, surrounded with angels and archangels and saints from every age and race and occupation. There would be a platform for the pulpit; the word would be preached, and in word and sacrament heaven would be brought down to earth and earth lifted up to heaven. Feeding and cleansing are spiritual as well as physical needs. Christ came into the world, living in a home for thirty years, to bring feeding and cleansing to the whole man. The Word is to become flesh in the Church, which is the extension of the Incarnation. In the sacraments of Baptism and Communion Christ is cleansing and feeding us, and in the Communion the holy and the common are brought together. We come to the parish church to Parish Communion to remember Christ and to become the Body of Christ—'This is My Body,' 'Ye are the Body'—inside and outside the parish church. In the parish church on the Lord's day we assemble together to claim the parish for Christ, and this has driven us bit by bit out of the parish church on a weekday to claim the parish street by street and house by house for Christ. For three years we have celebrated Communion in two houses each morning for three mornings a week, along with a daily celebration in church. From Lent, 1955, onwards we have taken the daily celebration itself into the homes. I was most uncertain about this until we took the plunge, but from the first day I celebrated the daily mass in the house this seemed the answer to the question, 'What are the people of God meant to be doing on weekdays at the Eucharist?' On Sunday quite clearly the answer is Parish Communion. On weekdays the answer seems to be the house celebration.

In people's houses we celebrate in surplice and stole (we use vestments in the church building), with the people gathered round the family table. The rite used is the 1662 without the Creed and *Gloria* and with the Prayer of Oblation following the Prayer of Consecration. Since October, 1952, we have had a sermon at every celebration including the regular daily celebration, whether in church as it used to be or in the houses as it is now: here is a link between the worship of Sunday and that of the weekday, for on Thursday, Friday, and Saturday in the sermon we look forward to next Sunday's collect, epistle, and gospel respectively, and on Monday, Tuesday, and Wednesday in the sermon we look back in the same way. In the house we use the vessels and wine from the church building and water and bread from the house. Each person puts his own bread on the paten and we say together the Offertory Sentence: we also say together the Collect for Purity, the Prayer of Humble Access, and the Prayer of Oblation. We sit for most of the service, but stand for the gospel and offertory and from the *Sursum Corda* until after the Lord's Prayer. When it is done, and how it is done, is secondary to what is done; the Holy Communion in houses, the breaking of the bread at a more local level than the parish church.

'I feel now that my home is part of God's world.' The trade-union leader who said this after a celebration of Holy Communion in his house was experiencing the purpose of Christ's birth, life, and death, and the purpose of the breaking of bread and the shared cup.

Four students from an Orthodox seminary near Constantinople once came to our parish; they spoke hardly any English, but they recognized the Church in action in the Parish Communion and the house celebration; their word for what they saw was 'zoe'—'life'—the keyword in the renewal of the Greek Orthodox Church. In our parish church and in our homes we are to let the liturgy be splendid and full of meaning: we are to take the Eucharist back into life.

CHAPTER V

# THE CHURCH MUST MEET

WHERE can the Church be met? This question was asked in *Towards the Conversion of England*, the report of the Archbishops' Commission on Evangelism, 1945.

### THE MISSING HALF OF CHURCH LIFE TO-DAY

The fellowship of the Church is integral to the Gospel. But in the life of the ordinary parish church, though it is possible to see the people of God met for worship, where else can the fellowship of the Church be expressed and experienced? The worshipping community of Sunday seems during the week to be broken up into segregated Church organizations, divided up according to age, sex, interests, and the like. The question has to be faced: 'Where can the Church be met and known, otherwise than when it is sitting in its pews? . . .'

In some parishes the experiment is being tried of a church meeting where members of the Sunday congregation are invited to meet each other and discover their corporate responsibility. Some means should be sought whereby, in the ordinary round of parish life, that common meeting place may be provided which is no longer (or seldom) afforded by ordinary social circumstances, and yet *without which a worshipping congregation can never become a family*. Then, be it remembered that fellowship is never found by seeking it as an end in itself. Fellowship is the by-product of sharing in a common purpose, and of devotion to a common cause.

The operative words in this quotation are 'community' and 'fellowship.' Great men and saints have gone out from the worship of the Church and have done great things for Christ, but they have gone out as individuals. Often there has been very little realization of the Church as a community with a vocation.

The aim of the worshipping community to become a working and witnessing community remains remote unless the Church meets to deliberate together, to live its life out together as a family with all the shocks to mind and heart and spirit that that entails. Increasingly in this parish we became aware of how little we have known each other; and growingly we realized how often we have been unwilling to learn how to speak the truth in love and how often we have approached our worship and our witness almost entirely as individuals. In the early Church this sense of togetherness found its centre in the Eucharist. There they were aware of themselves both as a divine community and as a missionary fellowship. They also met together to rehearse what great things God had done and to rehearse what great things God had still to do in their midst (*Acts* iv. 27).

The worshipping congregation must realize its vocation to be a slow, steady leaven, growing under the discipline of the Spirit into a converting fellowship. As a result, both the worship of Parish Communion and the personal piety of individual Christians are seen to be inadequate and the regular gathering of the Church out of church becomes recognized as vital. It is imperative, if the congregation is to be trained to realize its missionary responsibility in the parish, that there should be a regular gathering of the Christian family in that place, to meet in a way which Dr. Oldham described as something half way between a prayer meeting and a parish whist drive!

This part of the plan which is envisaged in *Towards the Conversion of England* was in the mind of Archbishop Temple when he launched the Life and Liberty Movement, which was an attempt to give the Church the opportunity to fulfil its vocation in the life of the people and the nation. The Parochial Church Council was to be the way in which the leaders in the parish, both clerical and lay, could learn from each other and work out their vocation to be the Body of Christ. This leadership was to be a representative leadership and the Parochial Church Council was to be elected by a congregational meeting to exercise it.

It shall be the primary duty of the Council in every parish to co-operate with the incumbent in the initiation, conduct, and development of Church work both within the parish and outside.[1]

A parish meeting once a year is obviously not sufficient to give the fullest opportunity to help the Parochial Church Council to give a lead, nor for the Parochial Church Council to exercise this leadership of the congregation by the formulation of a parish policy. Parish policy ought to be something which every member of the congregation feels he is constantly helping to create and carry out. There is a tremendous need for a growing sense of togetherness about all the concerns of a healthy congregation. So many of them are usually delegated to the vicar or the treasurer or the Parochial Church Council, but the Church itself must have a mind on these concerns.

Let me give some examples. I believe that such a thing as the finances of the Church ought to proclaim the Gospel. There are those who feel that things like bazaars and whist drives are not a good way of financing a church. The Rev. Jim Wilson, in his book *Redemption of the Common Life*, supports these misgivings when he states:

Indirect giving is not a healthy method of financing the work of the Church. Sales of work and bazaars train people to use commercial methods of profiteering and to expect something in return for what they give to the Church. It also leads members of the Church to expect that the Church will be supported by those who don't use it. The Church becomes a commercial concern and one bazaar is no sooner over than the whole activity of the parish is taken up with preparing for the next. Many churches are like the barren

[1] *Handbook for Churchwardens and Church Councillors*, p. 51.

fig tree, concerned only with the effort to keep a few leaves over its head, to keep the church roof repaired, with no time for any other work. Jumble sales and whist drives are as bad. If we have any self-respect we shall pay for what we want, bringing our envelopes each week-end, and, if we are away from church on any Sunday, bringing the envelope for that Sunday as well: not asking any one who does not come to church to pay for what is our own concern.

It is obvious that this presents a very real challenge to the Christian congregation. But I believe that the most important thing is not whether or not we have a parish bazaar, but whether we realize that we must have a parish policy about Church finance as well as every other matter.

As an example of working out a policy, here is an extract from the report adopted by the annual meeting at Halton in 1950.

How often we are asked, 'What has the Church to say in face of our difficult times?' The answer is, as it has always been, that the Church wants us each and all to live by the grace of our Lord Jesus Christ, with the love of God in the fellowship of the Holy Ghost.

The prayer and the sacraments of the Church are the channels of the grace of our Lord Jesus Christ. The love of God is revealed to us in His Word, which the Church lives and teaches. The fellowship of the Holy Ghost is experienced in the local Christian community in which we live.

Our Parish Policy, therefore, is the way in which we live together and proclaim the truth of grace, love, and fellowship to the world. The particular pattern of Christianity to-day seems to be the Christian community—society—fellowship. Hence our Parish Policy emphasizes mainly the two great evangelical sacraments—Baptism and Communion—and our ways of working out and living out their meaning for our time. Of course, the full sacramental devotional life of the Church is always there for the faithful, but it is not through that alone that we can best take the Gospel to the world to-day.

WORSHIP. The Parish Communion, preceded by Mattins. This is the main act of Family Worship and is meant for all ages of the family; special provision is made for young children so that their parents are not cut off from worship.

There is also a celebration of Holy Communion at 7.30 a.m. each Sunday and daily celebrations through the week.

We cannot receive Holy Communion before being confirmed and classes in preparation for this are held every year; special arrangements are made to help adults who wish to be confirmed.

EVENSONG: completes our Sunday worship and in it we join in the traditional worship and teaching of the Church and give thanks for the Holy Communion.

PUBLIC BAPTISMS: are usually six times a year[1] 'When the most number of people come together' (Prayer Book), so that we can be present to be reminded of our Baptism and Christian profession and to receive the new members into the family.

MEETING: Every Wednesday is parish meeting night: this is the main gathering of the family to take further the fellowship of the Lord's Table. The parish meeting may discuss any aspect of parish life, e.g. evangelism, or the work of some special section; annual meetings of such sections may take place on parish meeting night (e.g. the annual meeting of the Scouting and Guiding Parents' Committee, or the annual missionary meeting); speakers may be invited to make a special contribution.

The first Wednesday in the month is the meeting of the Parochial Church Council. This is the elected body of the people to consider their wishes and to 'co-operate with the Incumbent in the initiation, conduct, and development of Church work both within the parish and outside.' The Parochial Church Council is elected by those on the Electoral Roll at the annual parochial church meeting held in Easter week; it is the duty of all those on the Electoral Roll to be present in order to vote and to receive financial and other reports.

The parochial church meeting may be called together at other times during the year to discuss matters of special importance.

The Parochial Church Council is the executive of the parish.

[1] Now quarterly.

EVANGELISM: Home meetings are held during two weeks and at other times as arranged during the year with the special purpose of bringing the Church to those who are still only on the fringe.

Work for the Church overseas is organized by the missionary committee meeting annually with a parish meeting. Our target for giving to Missions needs to be raised owing to the serious effect of devaluation on the Church overseas.

SERVICE: The local church should assume responsibility for meeting any social need—elderly, sick, young married couples, and so on.

ORGANIZATIONS: provide for the various sectional interests within the Church: some are only for members of the Church, others are open to all, and are a means of drawing new people into the fellowship.

CHILDREN: Children's Council, made up of teachers and leaders and parents. Kindergarten, Junior Sunday School, Company of St. Wilfrid, Scouts, Guides, Cubs and Brownies, junior club, choir: meeting annually with a parish meeting.

YOUNG PEOPLE: The Youth Council, made up of leaders and two members representing each organization: meeting annually with a parish meeting. Senior A.Y.P.A., junior A.Y.P.A., youth club, boys' club, boys' choir, Scouts, girls' club, choir, Guides, Junior Dramatic Society.

We hope that lads will stay in these organizations until their call-up, and after that will come back into senior A.Y.P.A. or another adult group or into positions of leadership.

SOCIAL: Social committee of representatives of organizations to plan programme of social events and undertake running of some of them: meeting annually with a parish meeting. Dramatic Society: meeting annually with a parish meeting.

MEN: Men's School of Religion: Meeting annually on men's work with a parish meeting.

CHOIR: Meeting annually with a parish meeting.

WOMEN: Mothers' Union, Young Wives, women's meeting (evening), women's whist drives (afternoon): meeting annually on women's work, with a parish meeting.

THE SICK AND ELDERLY: Healing fellowship and intercession scheme: meeting annually with a parish meeting. Holy Communion at home for those unable to get to church. Home meetings are held regularly.

PUBLICATIONS: Parish Magazine: meeting annually with a parish meeting. Parish Diary. Parish Year Book.

SPECIAL EVENTS: Consecration Festival—week-end of Christian leadership (May). Parish Retreat—week-end retreat at home (September). Parish holiday (August). Missionary week-end (July). Social evenings on special occasions. (There is normally a social event every Saturday evening, except during Advent and Lent.)

This, then, is the parish policy which we appeal to all those on the Electoral Roll to discuss and if necessary amend and adopt at the annual meeting. Every member should understand the policy so that he or she knows what the Church is trying to do and can, if necessary, explain it to others. The members of the Parochial Church Council are those who should understand it most fully and should be co-operating fully with the main activities—Parish Communion, public Baptism, parish meeting; hence the election of members of the Parochial Church Council is an important duty. All organizations play their part in the whole life of the parish, and it is always to Christ first and then to the parish that members owe their loyalty and not to the section, for the whole is greater than the part.

The recurrent word in that report is 'meeting.' In detail the policy has changed, but the significance of that word has grown through the years. As we have met as a congregation and in houses, we have discovered again and again what Martin Buber means when he says 'All real living is meeting.' We are discovering the Bible, too, in a new and vital way; we are discovering a new sense of togetherness in approaching the Scriptures. We find ourselves being gathered into Christ by the same Spirit Who was responsible for the acts of the Apostles. We can see a connection between: (1) before Whitsun: 'these all continued *with one accord* in prayer and supplication.' (2) Whitsun: 'And when the day of Pentecost was fully come, they were all *with one accord* in one place.' (3) Soon after Whitsun: 'They continued steadfastly in the apostles' doctrine and fellowship, and in breaking of bread, and in prayers. And all that believed *were together* and had all things common.' (4) Later: 'And when they had come and *gathered* the Church together, they rehearsed all that God had done with them'; and (5) later still, the Bishop of Ripon addressing the parish meeting at Halton in 1951: 'Don't think the parish meeting is some sort of stunt of your vicar—it is a recovery of what the Church is—a recovery of the Church as the people of God. The word translated "people" is "*laos*" from which we get our word "laity." We are all—bishop, priest, and congregation—members of the laity, called to be the people of God—the "*laos*" of God. We live out that life when we welcome new members in Baptism, when we share in the common meal at the Parish Communion, when we meet in the parish meeting to live out our parish family life.'

But the inquirer will want to know what happens at a parish meeting. One might answer like the radio announcer, 'Anything may happen, and probably will!' Anything may happen! This couldn't be more true as a description of a parish meeting. First and foremost the meeting of the congregation ought to be a gathering expecting things to happen—expecting the Holy Spirit to work—remembering that the Lord is at hand. It is one of the ways in which the congregation is to be ready to be used by God.

But a parish meeting can be the very special target of the devil. I once said in fun to a Parochial Church Council, 'I don't mind the devil getting into members of the Parochial Church Council, because if he didn't it would mean it was dead, but I wish he'd let me know which ones before the meeting!' The same is true of the parish meeting, and the devil's special target may well be the vicar. We must be prepared for anything if we are to take Christianity seriously, for it is very dangerous and highly explosive.

Thomas Carlyle said that there were a thousand people who think to one who *sees*. The parish meeting is one of the ways in which the people of God are to learn to *see* their vocation to be a redeemed and redeeming community. Once we 'see' the point of the parish meeting we must meet whatever happens. There is, so to speak, a divine imperative about it. We may find any particular gathering an absolute bore. We may think the discussion is puerile and the whole thing is getting nowhere. But the most important thing is never to give it up as hopeless because that is to refuse to act on what we 'see,' or at any rate on what growingly we are meant to see.

So often people say, 'If only . . .' But we must start from where we are and be prepared to be led where we ought to be.

Yes, we must start where we are. Ideally there should be no need to have a programme for the parish meeting. Ideally each week would be a following up of the Parish Communion on the Sunday, and be the inthrust of the Church of God into the weekday world. Ideally there is no need for organizations in the Church, for its worship and its meeting should be applied directly to action in the world—to go out into the world to serve God faithfully in the fellowship of the Church.

In practice there will be as many varieties of parish meeting as there are parishes, just as there are as many homes as there are houses in the parish, and they each have an individuality derived from the character of the people who live in them. So we must start with the people who will come to the parish meeting, however old or young or of whatever sex, and whatever the number may be. We must let anything be discussed, the bazaar, or the parish retreat, or Baptism, or the branch library, or public lavatories at the tram terminus. We must accept the Parochial Church Council that we've got and the parish that we've got and the organizations that we've got and the people that we've got and the vicar that we've got!

Our policy and our programme must be evangelistic. Our focal point in this parish is Wednesday night. Whether we can come every Wednesday or not (only the Parochial Church Council members may come on the first Wednesday of each month in any case) we all ought to feel that Wednesday parish meeting is ours, to discover increasingly what it means to be the Body of Christ. Our particular aim in one particular year was to relate the electoral roll, the Parochial Church Council, the diocesan conference, and the Church Assembly to the local church, and to try and help the organizations to see their place in the life and witness of the Church—to see the relationship between the whole and the part. In practice this meant that the Parochial Church Council met on the first Wednesday of each month as the near-executive of the parish, duly elected at the annual parochial meeting and given certain executive functions by the Enabling Act. (To the Parochial Church Council in particular, and to the congregation in general, is given the responsibility to 'co-operate with the Incumbent in the initiation, conduct, and development of Church work, within the parish and outside.') In addition to the annual parochial meeting three other gatherings were held to which members of the electoral roll received a personal invitation, on Baptism, children's work, parish programme. Also two meetings a year were held to hear reports and have discussions on the diocesan conference and there were two on the Church Assembly and its proceedings.

We also believe that the congregation will grow to 'see' itself as the people of God as they become increasingly a Bible-reading fellowship, and so appropriate notes were introduced every quarter at the parish meeting.

We also had annual meetings on children's work, Scouting and Guiding, youth work, men's work, women's work, service, child and home exhibition, publications, finance, United Nations Association, as well as two with the Free Church people. We had an annual meeting on the Church overseas with two missionary week-ends, which included Sunday evening parish meetings. This left eight Wednesdays unaccounted for: four of these were left for any extraordinary discussion, and four were in August when we had no meetings.

The actual framework of each meeting is the method of corporate mental action described in the *Unto a Full Grown Man* series, which I edited with the Rev. S. H. Evans. Sometimes we divide into groups to discuss questions and on other occasions to formulate questions, and sometimes we have open forum.

This programme inevitably varies from year to year and from month to month. The important thing is to have a parish policy; it is just as important that it should be adjustable so that we can be sensitive to the changing needs of the congregation and parish. In the next chapter there is the story of how we went out from the parish meeting to meet in homes, which meant that a good deal of time and attention was transferred from the parish meeting and that some of the items in the above programme no longer take place. But without our experience of the parish meeting there could have been no house-church, and the house-church has driven us back to study the place and necessity of the parish meeting. In this we have been helped most valuably by studying together *The Parish Meeting at Work* by Alan Ecclestone, Vicar of Darnall, Sheffield. No one in the Church of England to-day has done more than he has to help us to see that the Church must meet, and how, and why.

He says:

It has been said with justice that 'the failure of the Church to guide men in the field of morals has been chiefly due to the fact that in its corporate life at all levels there has been so little free discussion of all the problems. The pulpit can only help up to a point'; and because we have not been ready to give help to lay people by lay people nor to elucidate the concrete issues faced by them in the factory, the office, and the shop in some such gathering as the parish meeting it is small wonder that they tend to be largely indistinguishable from the world. It is the special business of the parish meeting to make possible week by week 'the free frank discussion touching the relevance of our faith to daily life.' It is quite certain that there will be differences of opinion, 'but if the Church is a fellowship in Christ, it should be able to carry within itself differences of opinion and the possibility of diverse judgements.'[1]

Yes, but what actually happens in the parish meeting? Here is an ordinary specimen of a detail of parish policy that couldn't be worked out at the annual meeting. The problem was, 'How are the members of the congregation to become aware of their responsibility for the newly baptized?' On July 26, 1953, in the middle of our missionary week-end, at the end of the Parish Communion eleven babies were baptized and welcomed into the family of Christ's Church. In spite of Baptism interviews, home meetings, rehearsals, and a Baptism in the face of the congregation, on the whole the parents and godparents gathered round the font could have come from Africa or India—they were a foreign body. How is the congregation to realize its responsibility for the baptized unless it meets to face this out?

The plan worked out by the Parochial Church Council and parish meeting was that in October, 1953, in fourteen homes where babies had been baptized recently there should be home meetings at 8 p.m., followed by house celebrations and, most important, that at each of these meetings and celebrations there should be a gathering of the regular members of the congregation; these would have been present at the public Baptism and would try again to bring home to the parents the concern of the Church for them and for their children. They would also bring home in that domestic setting the meaning of the Church as the Body of Christ, as the divine community, and of their need to live by grace, most especially as it is expressed in the breaking of the bread.

[1] op. cit., p. 40.

What is clear is that there ought to be a policy about welcoming new members into the family and that it is the common concern of the whole congregation. The parish meeting is where it should be worked out. Later on in the book you can read about how this policy was put into practice.

CHAPTER VI

## *THE CHURCH IN THE HOUSE*

WE have seen that the parish meeting is the carrying into the world of the worship which centres in the church building. At this parish meeting anything which is the concern of an individual is the concern of the family. But the parish meeting has to be carried a stage further. It has to get into the highways and byways. One way of doing this is by means of a cell.

The Christian cell is formed of not more than twelve people. It must be kept 'local,' 'down our street.' It is in no sense a 'parish meeting,' though it may do for our street what the parish meeting is doing for the parish, and it ought continually to be feeding the parish meeting. Such cells are outposts of the Church—centres of its life where the Church's vocation can be seen in terms of Puddlecombe Terrace and Jemima Row. The parish priest is welcome but never indispensable, for it is essentially a movement in your area and for your area.

It is this outgoing of the Church which has led us to a rediscovery of the Church in the house. Let me illustrate from what has been attempted in Halton. For ten years, following a Franciscan convention and children's mission, home meetings have been held to try and meet the people where they are. These home meetings were at first deliberately organized in two special weeks during the year to try and make some contact with the great body of people who have had their babies baptized and have never been seen in the church building since. Quite a number of people have seen that this is an outstretching of the Church, but have not seen that they ought to do more about it, even though some of them may have come to the home meetings.

If the Christian message means anything, it means God coming down and God stretching out to touch us where we are. There is nowhere that our Lord Incarnate would go that our Lord in the Holy Communion wouldn't go. So, let us take the Eucharist back into life, let us build up the Church in the house: 'Philemon and the Church which is in his house'; 'Aquila and Prisca and the Church which is in their house'—it is just as much a part of the Church as the Church in Corinth or the Church in Rome. The Church in Mr. Smith's house is just as much the Church as the Church in the parish church in Halton. So in October, 1949, we felt that something was needed, something more than just going into people's homes to meet and discuss. Very slowly and hesitatingly and with very real misgivings we began to have meetings in houses in the morning when we brought the Reserved Sacrament and asked some of the lapsed baptized to come and see people actually receiving Communion and hearing the Scripture and a sermon in that sort of homely friendly surrounding. Gradually it became clear that it was a celebration that was needed and not this bringing of the Reserved Sacrament to the house; so once again, with many misgivings, in two or three selected houses Holy Communion was celebrated with others invited to attend to see.

The Church is the great new thing breaking through; there it is, wherever two or three are gathered together in Christ's Name to do this in remembrance of Him, whether in prison cell, cathedral, kitchen, or parish church. In the kitchen there is the Church. There the new creation is to take place. There the new Jerusalem comes down out of heaven. There the Word becomes flesh. There is Pentecost. If the only church in the diocese was the cathedral, there would be large tracts of the diocese untouched by the Church. If the only church in a parish is the parish church there are large tracts of the parish untouched. In the very heart of the old order the Church is to be set to transform the common and the ordinary, to claim it for Christ.

Renewal means the rediscovery of the meaning of worship, and in all this the rediscovery of the meaning of the Eucharist is essential. The Eucharist is an action of Christ and His Church which is to reach out and to touch every part of life. Some people say the proper place for Communion is the church. There is a sense in which that is true: if we do not find Him somewhere in particular we shall not find Him anywhere. But there is a danger which we see if we substitute 'Christ' for 'Communion'; then the criticism would sound like this—the right place for Christ is the church building, yes, and keep Him there, don't let Him interfere with home life, working life, political life, recreation, keep Him out of this world, keep Him away from the real world in which we spend most of our time. But Christ *must* come in to it all. He *must* interfere. It is only 'interference' because we are blind, because we are sinners. He wants to gather together into one all things. This is coming home in Halton through the house-church.

What is happening is a revolution in the way we see things. In the last twelve years we have been praying for the parish street by street. I believe the house-church is an answer to this praying. Two particular theological pressures have brought about the house-church: one to connect Baptism and Communion, membership and worship, and the other to connect the two communities, the congregation and the parish. We have seen that Baptism for the many and Communion for the few is a contradiction in terms. It would have made nonsense to St. Paul. If the people won't come to the Parish Communion to see the point of it, we must take Communion to them.

That was why we took the Communion to houses; growingly we became convinced that we ought to make a great act of faith and run a mission with home meetings and house celebrations as the main approach to the lapsed baptized. Every day for the month of October, 1952, three house celebrations took place, two in houses and one in church on behalf of a particular street or area. In a hundred different homes we held house celebrations in the morning and home meetings in the evenings;[1] in them we met over 1,000 different people.

Only one of these house celebrations was in the house of unconfirmed people, but it became quite clear that we must do two things; one, take the Communion service to the houses of the unconfirmed to help them to see something of the meaning of Communion, even though they cannot receive the sacrament; they are much more likely to respond to the invitation to have a celebration in their own house than to come to a celebration in some one else's house. Two: it is obvious that for the vast majority of the lapsed baptized, morning, at whatever hour, is difficult or impossible, and if we are really going to help these people from where they are to where we want them to be, then it is in the evening that we must go to the house. We must have the house celebration in the surroundings of the evening home meeting. May I quote here from a letter from my former colleague, the Rev. R. D. A. Wouldham, Rector of Bolam, Northumberland, who stayed with the Little Brothers of Jesus of Charles de Foucauld in the Sahara in the autumn of 1953?

I have been staying out in the wilderness with the brothers and sisters who are nomads and follow the same life as the Arab nomads. One of the brothers looks after the sheep and goats. He even sleeps out in the open with them. Normally he is not back before sunset. He takes some food for the day and finds opportunity to read his Bible and meditate.

The priest celebrates Holy Communion each day. It is the flock of sheep and goats that regulates the time of the celebration. There is no time in the morning; as soon as the flock is astir the shepherd has to be off. Consequently the breaking of the bread awaits their return in the evening—

[1] Regular home meetings had taken place after the Franciscan mission led by Fr. Algy Robertson in September, 1947.

usually just after sundown. But what a wonderful setting for the Eucharist—at the end of a day's work so that it is all obviously a part of the offertory: it is in the evening when men and animals are relaxed and can give their whole attention to God.

The move to have evening house celebrations was parallel to the move to have Parish Communion in the evening on certain weekday festivals during the year. At a number of parish meetings we asked ourselves, 'What are the people of God meant to be doing on Maundy Thursday?' And again and again we came to the conclusion that we ought to gather as a family at a time when the Church could really meet as a body. In Holy Week, 1952, when our services were conducted by the Bishop of Knaresborough, he that day celebrated Parish Communion at 8 p.m., and people were urged to fast for two hours before the service. In 1953 we had Parish Communion on Ascension Day evening, and Monday, Tuesday, and Wednesday in Holy Week, as well as Maundy Thursday; in Lent, 1954, we extended this to a weekly Parish Communion on Wednesday evening, which proved to be of such value that it has become part of our regular weekday programme.

This arrangement in Holy Week I approached with more misgivings than anything else we have done here, but I can't think of anything which could have brought the whole challenge of Holy Week before the congregation more than this did. I am quite certain that a far greater number of the congregation than ever before realized that Holy Week ought to interfere with their other arrangements. Holy Week is to every year what Sunday is to every week.

There is an insistent theological pressure to link the Parish Communion with the parish community, so we have been learning to take it into the homes to discover a more local embodiment of the Church. This has been discovered particularly in two ways:

(1) Meetings in homes of the congregation monthly in the evening. This is the parish meeting in dispersion, meeting to be trained at this local level by the Holy Spirit, with house celebrations in the morning.

(2) Meetings with or without celebrations in the evening in the homes of people who are not regular worshippers: these are to bring the Church to the houses of the lapsed baptized, to develop a sense of mission on the part of the congregation, to get alongside and on speaking terms with those who are outside the worshipping community, to help the congregation to start where the parishioners are.

These two forms of the house-church we in Halton call the 'intensive house-church' and the 'extensive house-church,' 'us' and 'us-plus,' respectively. Our policy at the moment is that in each month there shall be a week of each kind. Here is a way in which the congregation can be trained to be a mission station. More and more men and women are needed as the house-church develops, more and more members of the congregation will have to take house services or home meetings and by so doing they will come to realize what it means to be the Church.

The Bishop of Sheffield was once taking a celebration in a big ward in a London hospital and afterwards one of the bed patients spoke to him. He told the bishop that he had never seen a Communion service before, and he had understood it and had been very moved by it. The operative word is 'seen' and the operative word in our discovery here has been 'see.' In the houses in Halton people have said, 'I *see* the connection between what goes on in church and what goes on outside now.' 'I *see* that God is concerned just as much with what goes on outside the church building as inside.' 'I *see* now that I can worship God in my working clothes.' 'I *see* my house as part of God's world now.'

What we have been discovering in the last twelve years here is that there is a great need to build up the

Church in the home. Père Hyacinthe, writing in France seventy years ago, said something which is equally true in this country to-day:

Family religion is no more. There is individual religion; and if you take the members of your family one by one, or the best of them, you will find in the secret sanctuary of the conscience a flame, or at least a spark; but there is no longer a family altar where they pray and sing together. The remedy, my friends, I know it and I offer it to you. Rebuild the family altar! Have the courage to believe, to teach, to pray, to gather about you your wife and your children.

When we have families worshipping in their homes, bringing babes to Baptism, children to instruction and Confirmation, young people to marriage, and all to Communion, more and more the church will be the Church.

The house-technique, of course, implies small numbers, but that will not deter those who have learned the lesson of Gideon (*Judges* vii. 4) or the warning against ecclesiastical arithmetic in 2 Samuel xxiv. 10. The 'house' may indeed be what has long been sought under the name of the 'cell'—a term too ideological, biological, penal, or monastic to make a good label. If we can gather groups of resistance and loyalty in the hinterlands of apathy, whether in the village or the city, the day may come when we can unite them to march forward together. Whether we can do this seems to depend a good deal on whether, in a 'day of small things' we can work out the 'small' technique. We have given a fair trial to 'mass' techniques, and the results have often been unaccountably disappointing, despite all the spiritual impulse and imagination that have been behind them. If, as some may think, we have not at the moment the resources sufficient to influence greatly the nation or the community, may it not be worth while to consider the 'domestic' technique, in the hope that it will lead to bigger things?[1]

How have we tried to put this into effect in Halton? In September, 1953, the parish magazine carried a

[1] J. R. Lumb, *The Church Teaching Quarterly*, Michaelmas, 1952.

major announcement to show that this is not something that we are just talking about, but something that we are trying to do.

### The Parish Church and the House-Church

There is a mission going on all the time in the parish. The effectiveness of that mission depends to a large extent on how far the congregation realizes its vocation to the mission. Every parish is a mission field and the local congregation with its building, its services, its P.C.C., its organizations, is the centre from which mission work is to be effected. To-day in the parish there is a need to take the offensive. In September and October we are taking the Church out into the streets and homes of our parish. Whatever we may think about the programme for September and October if we haven't any better way of tackling the mission field in this parish then let us all say our prayers and take our place in this task. It is not a question of 'if you please,' for we are under orders from our Lord to go into all the world, which includes our own parish.

In the normal month the worshipping community here meets each Sunday morning at 9.30 a.m. and at Evensong at 6.30 p.m., and that is taken into the week as follows:

1st Week: through P.C.C., home meetings for elderly people, for men, and through organizations.

2nd Week: through the house-church on the Wednesday, house celebrations each morning, through home meetings for women, for young people, and through organizations.

3rd Week: Parish meeting on Wednesday, home meetings for elderly people, and organizations.

4th Week: The house-church each night at 8 p.m., and through organizations.

In September there is a special series of home meetings for children, in preparation for the new session of children's work, and a special series of youth home meetings to prepare for the new session of young people's work. In October and November we shall be continuing our special series of people's services at 6.30 p.m. each Sunday, beginning with the Harvest Festival on October 4th. (Evensong and public Baptism will take place on October 4th at 3 p.m., otherwise Evensong will be said at 6 p.m. during these months.) In the fortnight following the Baptism, fourteen home meetings and house celebrations are being held in homes where one or both of the parents are unconfirmed, thus bringing the Church to their homes and helping them to see where Communion comes into their lives. In November we are doing the same in homes of those who have been married in our church. During each week celebrations of Holy Communion will take place daily in the church building with additional celebrations on saints' days.

There follows the parish diary, which contains not only services in church and meetings in the hall, but also a complete list of all house meetings and house celebrations, with names and addresses given in each instance. All members of the congregation are urged to attend at least one of them. The congregation is not allowed to think of itself as just a group of people who go to a church building. With the Parochial Church Council it is challenged to bring the fellowship of the Church to all people. One has seen in these house celebrations and home meetings elderly people and lonely people having a new sense of their place in the fellowship of the Church, not least their place in praying for the building up of the kingdom of God in our parish. One has seen elderly people who are a bit queer become less queer because the fellowship of the Church has come to their house and to their street in a new and vital way.

The Parochial Church Council and the congregation are not allowed to forget the Church's children; so in twelve homes in September the Church goes out to show the concern of the Church for her children, and to see how natural the medium of a home is for teaching. (We showed the film strip of the coronation and played the record in about thirty children's homes in the fortnight before the coronation, and I am certain that in at least these thirty homes parents realized something of what the Church was trying to do for her children.) In September we took a film strip of a Communion service which we had used at the adult meetings; we also brought the

Communion vessels, wine, and wafers from church; we laid the table for tea, then we showed how we would 'lay the table' for the Lord's Supper in the same way. House celebrations have been especially arranged for mothers and children and how wonderful it is to celebrate Communion in houses with the little children quite naturally taking their part in this sacrament of Christ's love, though not, of course, receiving the elements. Here is the visual aid that, please God, many of them will never forget. They will grow up in an environment in which Communion is a vital experience of their earliest days in their home. I am quite certain that these celebrations are encouraging family prayers and we are seeing the truth of the slogan, 'The family that prays together stays together.' It is in the same way that special meetings for men, for young people, and for women, including special ones for young wives, all provide ways and means in which the Church may come to the people where they are and lead them, please God, from where they are bit by bit right into the very centre of the worshipping community.

So with the special series in October for parents who have had their babies christened in church, and in November for those who have been married in church, we provide an opportunity of letting the church be the Church. I believe that either we must stop baptizing infants, or we must help people who have been incorporated into the Church in Baptism to come to realize something of what it means to live by grace—to help them to discover Communion as the central act of the Church and the centre of their lives. I believe, too, that either we must stop marrying people in church who are not communicants, or we must help those who are married in church to see that the Church's blessing on their marriage can only be fulfilled in so far as they take their full part in the Church's central act of worship.

But central to all these 'extensive' meetings in the homes are the monthly 'intensive' home meetings of the regular members of the congregation for Bible study, prayer, discussion, and Communion. It is here that the regular Church people get alongside their missionary task. Here they get alongside in a way they can never get alongside by occupying a seat in church. Here they are learning to study the Bible together and letting the Bible come alive by doing it together. Here they are learning to lead by leading, here they are learning to pray by praying together. Here is the means whereby Church members are to be trained, trained out in the frontier where the main task of evangelism is to be done. This is the result of theological pressure, for surely the whole point of the Word becoming flesh was that God came into His own creation to get alongside men in the everyday home and work situation. If the saying is true that an Englishman's home is his castle, and the majority of those castles are unrelated to the parish churches of our country, then I believe it is in keeping with the mission of the Incarnate Lord that we should knock at the doors of these people; yes, more—we should beat on the doors of these people and ask them home by home if they are prepared to offer a table in their home so that the central act of the Church's life may be celebrated on it, so that they may come to realize the love of God, the God Who for their sakes and for our sakes, for their salvation and for our salvation, came down from heaven and lived and died and rose from the dead, and lives and reigns and will come again in glory.

It is true that the house-church is presenting anew the challenge of being the Church. At the house level some questions about the Church come alive in a new way. How are we to help those who are outside the worshipping community to become active members of the Church? How are we to help those who have been made members of the Church in Baptism to become active members of the worshipping and witnessing community? Many of those people for whom Christ died think of Church people as those who make a hobby of Communion—'Your hobby's Communion, mine's pigs!' The Church as the Body of Christ becomes very relevant in the street when it meets in a house in the street. The Church is the Body of Christ as exposed in its weakness and its strength at the house level. It is much more out on the frontier that one experiences the weakness and the strength of the Church as the Body of Christ. At the house level one realizes in a fresh way the risks Christ took, God took, when the Word was made flesh and dwelt among us. Surely there is nothing more helpless, more dependent on others, than a new-born babe, and this is what God did for us men and for our salvation. The manger is the extent to which God is prepared to go. His identification with us men was epitomized in the Cross; the symbol of shame was the symbol of strength through weakness; the Church is His Body and in that Body we experience the weakness of Christ which is our strength, and we experience all too often our own weakness, which is very weak.

In the Old Testament the idea of the holy was removed from the common. This was symbolized in the Temple. The outer court for the Gentiles and the next part for Jews only, then for the priests only, then the holy of holies, in which only the high priest could enter, and that only once a year. In Christ there is brought together both senses of the word 'holy.' Here is attachment to the world and detachment from the world held together in the person of Jesus Christ, with all the cost of manger and Cross. He took our human flesh, poured Himself out, and the night before He suffered when He was trying to explain the meaning of His Cross and Passion, the meaning of His coming and the meaning of His going, He took bread and wine after supper. He took this common thing off the table and said the most staggering thing—'This is My Body, this is My Blood'; and the price of this involvement of Christ in the common things is the Cross.

The next time He broke bread was not in the next world or in a huge mansion, but round a table after the walk to Emmaus. He was known to them in the breaking of bread. Here is the kingdom. Here is the whole meaning of His coming to consecrate the ordinary, to redeem the secular. In Communion we see ordinary things change; in Communion we see ordinary people made strong; in Communion the kingdom comes. Communion is the great act of the Church. It is the great act of Christ in His Church claiming the world as His own—reclaiming it. Communion reminds us that the Church is not a building, but a community. It is encouraging to find what we have discovered, pastorally, supported by Dr. John Robinson, in his article in *Theology* in August, 1950.[1]

What I want to do is to consider the relation which should exist between two levels of this Church-existence, between the Church as it comes to expression 'at Corinth' and as it reproduces itself 'in thy house,' or, in modern terms, between the parish Church and the cell—or house—Church.

The parish Church (and, needless to say, I am using 'Church' here and throughout to describe not a building but a community) is something that is perfectly familiar. But the idea of the house-Church is one that needs clarifying.

There are two mistakes we can make in our thinking at this point, both of which derive from an untheological attitude of mind. The first mistake is to think of the house-Church as a purely temporary expedient: a makeshift arrangement characteristic of the earliest Church in Jerusalem or in any other mission area, an organization which serves until the parish Church can be constituted. (This line of thinking very soon betrays the insidious identification of the parish Church with a building of bricks and mortar.) And the second error is to think of the house-Church simply as an evangelistic weapon, a technique for getting at those on the frontier not yet ready to accept the full Christianity of the parish Church. It is, as it were, a half-way house for the semi-converted—taking Christianity into the home or factory,

[1] This article is printed by kind permission of the editor of *Theology.*

through that later to pass men on to the full sacramental life of the Church.

But both these conceptions are untrue to the New Testament. For it, the Church in the house is not an *ad hoc* expedient: it is a theologically necessary part of the life of the Body. When St. Paul writes: 'Aquila and Prisca salute you much in the Lord, with the Church that is in their house'; or, from the other end, 'Salute Prisca and Aquila . . . and the Church that is in their house'; or, 'Salute the brethren . . . and Nymphas, and the Church that is in their (RVM: her) house,' he is not implying that these people were working in mission areas where a 'parish' had as yet not been established (the places mentioned are in fact such well-settled centres as Ephesus, Rome, and Laodicea); not that these were semi-Christian outposts of the faith. He means, rather, that these were Churches within the parish Church, as to-day the parish Church is a Church within a diocese. Each colony of Christianity was honeycombed with smaller units.

This idea of the cellular structure of each parish, reflecting exactly the cellular structure of each diocese, is something that has been grievously lost in the modern Church. We should never think of a diocese being an agglomeration of individuals or a federation of local organizations (such as the Mothers' Union or the Church Lads' Brigade), but always as an organic union of parishes. But on the smaller scale that is precisely how we are content to think. Our parishes are for the most part collections of individuals; or, if these are brought together, it is in organizations. These latter are not units of the whole Church in miniature, but sectional groupings founded on some specifically limited basis of sex, age, or shared interest. No one could possibly call them Churches, though they often try to act like Churches, and we have the theologically obnoxious practice of corporate Communions for special organizations and societies—as though anything other than a Church could celebrate the Eucharist. By contrast, the house- or cell-Church is essentially of the same mixture as the lump, except that the area of natural community is smaller (e.g. a street group) and may, in these days when communities are often not geographical at all, be outside the parish altogether (for instance, in an office or factory).

I believe that the theological recovery of this notion of the Church in the house (and again I do not mean primarily bricks and mortar; for the group may meet in the church building) is one of the most important tasks of our generation. Whereas the organization is an optional extra, I believe that the cellular structure of the Church will be rediscovered as a necessity of its life. It was what John Wesley meant when he insisted that every Methodist—that is to say, every methodical Anglican—must be a member of a class meeting. It is the kind of thing that is being reborn, this time outside the parish Church, in the movement of the Spirit described in *France Pagan.* But the danger is that we shall miss the real theological significance of it all. . . .

Within the Body it has a function which is irreplaceable. This can be described best, perhaps, in terms of the Johannine metaphor. The house-Church represents, so to speak, the tap-roots of the vine, the Church underground, that of the life of the tree most closely in contact with the clinging soil of everyday existence: it is the tree as it is embedded in the deepest crevices and seams of the secular world. The cell-Church is what feeds new life into the parish Church, as the innumerable tap-roots nourish the stock of the vine. And then, from the parish, the Church can throw out its leaves and fruit in the great dioceses and provinces which cover the earth, and rear its head in the heavenly places as 'the general assembly and Church of the first-born.' But without the cell- or house-Church it becomes like those trees whose roots are all visible above the ground, and which are fast losing living contact with the soil, either to take anything out of it or to put anything back into it. . . .

The cell-Church, being the Church as it is in the house, must reproduce the whole life of the Body, all the 'marks' of catholicity—the Apostles' teaching and fellowship, the breaking of bread and the prayers. The first and the last, in the form of groups for Bible study and prayer, are well accepted marks of the Church in the cell. What I want to say will be concerned solely with the second—namely, the breaking of the bread. For the Eucharist is, *par excellence*, the pattern-action of the Church, that by which the *Koinonia* is constituted and by which it is to be recognized, whether it be in a cathedral or a Gestapo prison. One should not be able to come across the Community at any level without finding the Communion.

At once, I suppose, we are faced with the objection: 'But how can a bit of the parish celebrate the Holy Communion? How can a few people, a house, take upon themselves the action of the whole Church?' That only goes to show how awry our doctrine of the Church has got. Ask another question: 'How can the parish celebrate the Eucharist?' To us that seems obvious. But it was far from obvious to the Church of the early centuries, which inclined to hold that only the diocesan Eucharist, at which the bishop presided, could be valid. But that difficulty was overcome by the recognition that at every Eucharist, at whatever level, the whole Church is celebrating; and hence the prerequisite that a priest must preside, ordained and authorized as he is by the bishop to act in the name of the universal Church of God. It is always the Church which celebrates, be it the Church in the diocese, in the parish, or in the house. It is significant, perhaps, that when, on a recent occasion, I talked of the Christian community celebrating the Eucharist in the house, I was at once suspected of advocating lay celebration. So little do we remember to-day that the action of the Eucharist is always, at every level, the Christian community celebrating through the priest, and not the priest celebrating for a congregation.

The only way back is to apply here all the theology of the Sunday Parish Communion and to rediscover the weekday Eucharist as *par excellence* the celebration of the Church in the cell, in the house. This would mean (and here I am deliberately flying a theological kite) that the present individualistic low mass must become gradually superseded by a number of house celebrations, most probably in the evening, all of which would be gathered up in the Parish Communion on Sundays. It is for such a priesthood that we ought perhaps more and more to be training—and, maybe, rethinking our whole conception of the ministry. Where these celebrations take place—in the church or in the home—is largely irrelevant: it is the community that celebrates them that is important. But to such an extent have we lost our roots in the soil that the only way to recover the integral connection of the eucharistic offering with daily work may be to take the whole thing right back into the midst of the sweat and muck it is meant to be offering and transforming.

Here are a few lines from a description of a mass celebrated at the end of a day by a priest-workman in a docker's home in France. 'More beautiful than the flowers were the careful but heavy genuflections of this priest who had been working all day at the docks and whose movements evidenced the weights he had been carrying. The mystery of the Redemption is taking place at the very spot where it is needed. Outside, the seven children of the Valès family are playing, and when after our thanksgiving we meet in the court all hung with drying linen and old blankets being aired, life seems new to every one.'

It is when the Eucharist is really taken back into life that we shall begin to rediscover many, many things we have forgotten. At the parish level, and still more at the cathedral level, it is bound, like every large-scale social action, secular or sacred, to become formal and stylized. That is how it should be. But that is a healthy development only if we are at the same time, at the level of the house-Church, knowing something which is not formal but genuinely spontaneous. We should clearly be missing something vital if the only meal we ever knew was a boiled-shirt dinner party or a Lord Mayor's banquet. . . .

Let me end where I began, by insisting that all this must be seen as a theological rediscovery. It is not merely a technique for getting people into the Church, vitally important as it is at that. The cell is itself the Church, the Church in the basement, at the molecular level, in the smallest possible unit of Christian existence, whether it be among the dockers at Corinth or theological students at Wells.

Dr. Robinson's statement gives a full theological justification for the house-church which has already proved so valuable here in Halton. But what of the future?

There are about one hundred streets in this parish, and in the next five years our policy is to build up the house-church in every one of them. This would mean at least 1,000 people meeting regularly in the home to 'continue steadfastly in the apostles' doctrine and fellowship, and in breaking of bread, and in prayers.' How can we bring this about in our own homes in the parish—in the thousands of homes of couples who have been married in the Church of England, whose babies have been baptized at the fonts of the Church of England, who have been confirmed by the bishops of the Church of England, who attend the organizations of the Church of England, but to whom the Church and its mission mean little or nothing?

I believe we must take the Church into the home. We must help the mothers *and* fathers to teach their children what it means to belong to the Church. Parents know what it means to belong to their own home; let us help them to know what it means to belong to the Church, by teaching them to belong to the Church in their own house. They know what it means to believe in each other. We must help them to know what it means to behave in their own home in a certain way. We must teach them what it means to pray and to read the Bible and to worship. I believe they will learn this by discovering and rediscovering the Church which is in their house. They will learn to relate the Bible to everyday life as they break bread from house to house, as they eat their food with gladness, as the Lord adds to the Church daily such as should be saved.

The centre of the Church Catholic is the bishop, and the diocese is the basic unit of the Church. In the Anglican Church in this country the Church in each diocese is divided into parishes. Parishes are not of divine ordinance, but they are certainly necessary if the Church in the diocese is to be built up in more local areas than the diocese. We do not think of the diocese as made up of the Mothers' Union, the C.E.M.S., the Church Lads' Brigade. We think of the Church in the diocese as consisting of parishes, parish churches. But in the parish we have organized our life outside worship, very largely through organizations. So when we supplement what goes on in the parish church we do it normally through organizations. Organizations can help, although many to-day would ask whether organizations do, in fact, effectively bring people into the worshipping community or whether they often do just the reverse. Whatever may be true of organizations and whatever may be done in the parish church or hall, I believe there is a divine imperative to go out and build up the Church at the house level. I believe that when this is done we shall find the Church becoming more alive in the parish church and in the homes of our people. I am sure that Mary Sumner, the founder of the Mothers' Union, was right when she said, over fifty years ago,

> Let us settle it in our hearts that the greatest work we can do for the nation is to strive to bring the Church into the home; which means Christ Himself into hearts and homes. . . . Christ must be in every home, if it is to be in any way a home of peace and love. . . .
>
> . . . God's plans are better than our own, and He has ordained that the training place for His human creatures should be the home; the training place for parents as well as children. . . .

The Mothers' Union, when it is loyal to its objects, can help to do just this thing, but by and large I believe it is failing to do so; and so are other organizations, because the Church organized from the parish church and through organizations, however good they may be, cannot cope with establishing the Church in the parish as a whole.

I quote from Dr. Robinson's letter in *Theology* (August, 1953):[1]

> I shall not attempt to describe what I saw at Halton, except to say that one found the Church living at a level at which she can seldom have lived since the days of the Acts. The breaking of bread from house to house and the rediscovery of the *Ecclesia* of God in all its fullness at basement level—these can be described only by sharing in them and by

[1] This is printed by kind permission of the editor of *Theology*.

listening to the unaffected testimony of men and women who owe to them their knowledge of Christ and a Churchmanship vivid and articulate, often concealed from the wise and prudent.

If the altar in church is to be rediscovered for the majority of people in this country I believe they must first discover it at their own hearths. We must capture the homes of our country for Christ. Here is a mission that is straightforward, that is obvious, that is relevant—powerfully relevant. The Church is to be, and indeed in some measure it is, a redeeming, a reconciling community. Baron von Hügel said that the sacred goes bad if it has not the secular to work on. If the Church is not redeeming the world the Church goes bad. Studdert Kennedy said that we can fill our sanctuary with lilies and have the most wonderful reredos (and the right number of candles) and the choir can sing the most heavenly anthems, but if the Cross has lost its redemptive power then the whole thing stinks and God can smell the stench through it all! The Church is totally committed to redeem the world, including the world of politics and economics, and the more it becomes truly Catholic and believes in the Holy Spirit, the more it will lead the world into all kinds of truth.

The most important thing about us is that we are baptized. It is this belonging to the Church, belonging to Christ in the Church, that is our fundamental profession, and upon this profession alone can fully be built any other profession whether it is mother or father or butcher, baker, candlestick maker. In our vocation our main calling is to go out into the world to serve God faithfully in the fellowship of the Church; this involves us in relating the Church to every one and everything. This could never be dull, although it is sometimes hard and grim.

Our membership in the Church, our Christian profession, is expressed most characteristically in the family meal, the Holy Communion. This is for every one or it is for no one. That this great evangelical sacrament which is meant to relate the holy and the common, which is meant to teach man the truth about God and the truth about man and the truth about bread, should have become so hedged in that only very few of the baptized ever receive Communion is indeed a disastrous misunderstanding.

Every one is meant to be present at the Lord's Supper. There is an invitation to all; the Church is not responsible for getting every one present, but it is responsible for seeing that every one gets the invitation. Here is the mission of the Church. Here is the mission of the two evangelical sacraments. How right Bishop Azariah was to get his Indian congregations to put their hands on their heads and to say together as a slogan, 'I am a baptized Christian. Woe is me if I preach not the Gospel.' This could be the slogan of every home.

What is the real situation in the country as a whole? Here is an illustration from a country parish. There is a parish church with a population of about 1,200. There is a good parish priest and he works from his parish church, which is on the top of a hill in the centre of the parish: and there are half a dozen hamlets at the bottom of the hill scattered round the edge of the parish. A few people come to the parish church for Communion daily and a few more on Sunday at 8 a.m. A few more attend the Sung Eucharist at 11 a.m., and there are a handful at Evensong. The question the parish priest and the faithful ask—why don't the people come to church? Of course, some of them don't come because of sin and laziness, but many don't come because what goes on in church is foreign to them, absolutely foreign. We must realize just how far they are from the worshipping community—how far they are from the idea of the vocation of the Church to be the Body of Christ—how far they are from the idea of their supernatural destiny. It is no use saying they ought to come. They have no intention of coming. They wouldn't know what to do if they did come, even those who have gone to Sunday school, even those who have been confirmed, and gone regularly to church before their marriage and lapsed for five, ten, or twenty years: something has happened to them which makes the step into the worshipping community very difficult.

Archbishop Temple has translated 'In My Father's house are many mansions' as 'In My Father's house are many resting places.' I believe in a parish we must supply many resting places for people on the way into the heart of the worshipping community. In the country parish I mention above, it is the way the priest and the faithful look at the parish that is inadequate. If these hamlets were seen as outposts of the Church and a house-church built up in each of the hamlets (and not a chapel of ease or a mission church!) then the Communion could be celebrated on Sunday or on a weekday, whichever was most possible, and that would be the occasion for being the Church most characteristically in that part of the parish. Perhaps on certain occasions a couple of buses could be hired to go round the hamlets to pick up all the house-church folk and bring them up to the parish church and parish Eucharist. Afterwards there could be a great parish breakfast; a real social occasion could be made of it. In certain parishes one could imagine this being done in the evening with a real parish supper to follow. It may be that increasingly we shall discover that it is better to receive the Communion as a parish in the evening rather than continue with the few or relatively few in the morning, particularly on a weekday. The Pope has made quite clear his view that it is far more important to receive Communion than to receive Communion fasting.

No amount of special services, special conventions and missions, visual aids, and so on will bring home to the bulk of our people the meaning and challenge of the Church; but in the domestic situation in the surroundings of the home, the Church can be built up, the Church can be renewed, the Church may become real to the lapsed communicant. This will involve more leadership, ordained and unordained, and it will demand a new strategy in the use of clerical manpower. We need more priests but we need priests in teams even more. We need priests and we need laymen—a new kind of layman who is alive to the Christian principles and is concerned for God's sake to be doing his daily work and to witness in his trade union or employers' association and in politics.

When the congregation meets by the dozen in dispersion in five or ten houses of regular worshippers to study the Bible, to pray together, to discuss together, and to be concerned about their neighbourhood, the Church becomes the Church in a way it can never do at the parish church.

When the congregation meets in dispersion in five or ten houses of non-worshippers or lapsed worshippers in different parts of the parish the people of God are not discussing any longer how to contact the outsiders, they are meeting in the houses of outsiders.

When the congregation meets in dispersion in five or ten houses in different parts of the parish to meet other Christians we are not discussing the Ecumenical Movement in theory, we are not just discussing the findings of one of the World Conferences or Councils, we are learning to get alongside each other at the ground level. In our houses we are learning that in Christ there is no one we haven't something to learn from. When the congregation meets in dispersion in five or ten houses in different parts of the parish to be present or to conduct services for sick or elderly people or for any other people who find it difficult to come to the church building, the people of God are being trained to exercise their common priesthood. When the congregation goes out two by two to houses to conduct Sunday school classes, or goes out to visit those being prepared for Confirmation in houses or to attend or conduct prayer meetings or healing services in a house, or to bring the Church to the house in any other way that the congregation sees fit, the Church is becoming the Church, the Church is exercising its priesthood and claiming the whole of life for Christ.

With the development of the house-church here there has come a new sense of belonging. Baptism is being rescued from superstition and individualism, and it is no longer felt tolerable that people should be baptized and not have the challenge of Communion put to them by the Church going out in the context of the Communion service to proclaim the fullness of Christian initiation. We have come to a new sense of togetherness, we belong to each other and therefore we want to do things together. We come together to baptize because we are the community in which Christ baptizes, we come together to break bread because we are the community in which Christ breaks bread and we come together to bear witness because we are the community in which Christ is to witness. A miner who had never been to church in his life before, three days after a Communion service in his house asked to be prepared for Confirmation, and a house Confirmation class was held in his house. An invalid who has been receiving Communion for ten years, reserved at the celebration in his parish church, became one of the power houses of the parish through the Church going to his house.

The congregation can also meet in dispersion to get alongside people not as Christians but as fellow citizens, whether Conservative, Socialist, or Communist, whether Jew or Gentile, whether Roman Catholic, Anglican, or Free Church, to meet each other as people, to provide an environment in which Christians can listen and learn from non-Christians, and non-Christians can listen and learn from Christians. Here is the Church claiming the world, here is the Church cradling democracy. Over a thousand years ago Theodore of Tarsus introduced the parish system in this country as the best way of building up the Church in the diocese under the bishop. The parish system is still an essential way of building up the Church, but there is a need for more local manifestation of the Church. In the house-church we have discovered the meaning of worship and mission with fresh reality and relevance, and in it we are discovering the need for a new kind of layman and a new kind of ordinand.

## CHAPTER VII

# *THE CHURCH TEACHING*

THE congregation in general and the parents, godparents, and Sunday school teachers in particular must be vitally concerned with teaching the Church's children. There is a need to awaken the Church out of her lethargy about her children, and that can best be done as each local congregation becomes aware of its vocation to be the Church.

But how can we have a common policy, how can we work towards a common concern, unless we meet to do so? The congregation as a whole should be concerned about the affairs of every section. The smallest parish meeting we have had at Halton was one to discuss children's work. The congregation didn't turn up because they thought it was no concern of theirs; the parents didn't turn up because most of them were not vitally interested, provided that John and Mary had somewhere to go on a Sunday. The teachers didn't turn up because they didn't really feel it was the concern of the congregation! One part of the family does not know what the others are doing. Few people are concerned about the Church's work with her children unless their own children are involved or unless somebody breaks a window! And if they have so little concern for what is happening inside the church building they are not likely to be very concerned about the hundreds of children that are made members of the Church in Baptism but never come anywhere near the parish church.

Confirmation preparation begins at the font, as Canon A. R. Browne-Wilkinson reminds us:

> The whole teaching strength of the parish is called into action on behalf of every child baptized, and this with

Confirmation and subsequent life as a communicant clearly in view the whole time. The Prayer Book does not envisage a desultory and quite unfocused period of religious education in childhood, to be followed by a sudden concentration on Confirmation towards the end of childhood. On the contrary, all the years of childhood are to be years of deliberate preparation for Confirmation; this is to be the principle of focus and coherence. . . . The intention of the Prayer Book is frustrated unless the parish priest ensures that all Sunday school teaching is a true part of the preparation for Confirmation. There may be other auxiliaries such as club leaders and scout and guide officers; their task is not directly religious instruction, but it is very definitely religious nurture and care that 'they may grow up in Thy constant fear and love.'[1]

One of the most important aims in our church work is to help the congregation to feel that the Church's children are their children. We jointly have a responsibility to place the Church's children in the sort of environment in which they look forward to Confirmation and to full communicant life. One of the ways in which this can be done is by using the means provided in the parish church. If parents would drop into the parish church—in fact, into any church that they were passing—children would grow up to feel that this is the thing to do. If the child learns to crawl about, to talk and to walk and to ask questions in the church, the church building itself will become part of his natural environment.

It is right that the child should become familiar with the church building as the family house and as the house of prayer, outside the times of church services, but it is also important that the child should become knowledgeable about the Communion service by being present.

The two biggest revolutions that take place in a person's life are marriage and when a family comes. Most of the people who have their children baptized have never been regular communicants themselves, and therefore it is not very likely that they will see any point

[1] *The Prayer Book Way of Preparation for Confirmation.*

in being regular after these two revolutions take place. The local congregation has a responsibility to help them and their children to become regular communicants. Each parish must work out a policy about building up the worshipping community, family by family.

The policy at Halton is to have a nursery for the under-threes, so that parents can come to worship together. Until September, 1955, from three to seven years old the children came in to the service up to the Creed, then they went into the hall for kindergarten. After seven they were encouraged to stay in for all, or more and more of the Parish Communion. If the parents do not attend, the children over seven are encouraged to attend Parish Communion with a teacher or a leader or another adult member of the congregation. From September, 1955, the children from three to seven years go straight into the hall and are brought into church during the offertory hymn, and are encouraged to come up to the altar with their parents or friends to receive a blessing.

This is attempting to bring the parents from where they are to where we wish them to be, right in the very centre of the worshipping community. But when everything has been done that can possibly be done within the parish church, most of the people who bring their babies to be baptized, and even those who send their children to Sunday school and to church organizations, will never come into the centre of the worshipping community unless we do something else. The congregation must go out to the lapsed baptized.

A Spanish proverb says, 'An ounce of parent is worth a ton of priest.' And a pound of Sunday school teacher, club leader, or day school teacher! We must help the parents to accept responsibility. The parents should be helped to teach their children the Catechism. There is a fundamental inadequacy about a child learning to pray only at mother's knee. And there is an even more fundamental inadequacy if the child never sees father on his knees. It is here that the meaning of belonging to the Christian family is to be learned and experienced. In this we have found the house-church quite invaluable.

The other week here at the vicarage we had a house celebration, and there were sixteen children present under eight. When the cross and candles were placed on the dining-room table our son Peter, aged three, dashed upstairs to his mother and said, 'Church has come'; he rushed up again when the bread and wine were placed on the table, and said, 'The bread and the wine's ready.' I am not now arguing at what stage children should be encouraged to attend the Parish Communion, but even if they attend from infancy I believe that there is something which they catch from a celebration in the home which supplements their experience at the Parish Communion. At the Communion services with mothers and young children the children grow up familiar with the cross and candles, the church coming into their houses. They see the parish priest praying the prayers of the book, they see him taking the bread and wine in the consecration prayer, they see people holding up their hands to receive Holy Communion. They are accustomed to hear the Word of God read, the Word of God preached. They become familiar with the words of the service. These children will never have to be introduced to it as something foreign. They will not have to be told that Communion is related to everyday life. They will not need to be told that Christ comes into everyday life. They will have experienced it and they will be looking forward more and more to entering into the fuller life of the parish church and bit by bit will do so.

It only seems a step from the house celebration with mothers and children to a Sunday school in the house. I do not believe that the Sunday school movement orientated round a Sunday morning or Sunday afternoon instruction has a great deal of future unless it is supplemented by the house school and the house celebration. I believe Canon Lumb was right when he says

England is full of 'Sunday school Christians' who have never found their way to church, Confirmation, and the Eucharist because they thought that the Sunday schools had fed their 'minds' in childhood and they never went on to discover that they had 'souls' to be nourished.

We all know the long list of difficulties in building up a strong Sunday school and also the wearisome excuses given by parents for not sending or bringing their children to Sunday school. By taking the Sunday school into the street we are taking the mission of the Church out of the parish church into the street. One of the classes that we have started like this is being taken by a Sunday school teacher who is now forbidden for health reasons to come down to the church building twice on a Sunday. These schools are drawing in many children who were entirely out of touch with the parish church, who otherwise would come nowhere near us. One has grown so big that there is now a second class, meeting in the kitchen!

If these house-schools move around from house to house wherever possible, one is making a very real contact with homes and parents, particularly mothers. I visualize some of these parents being prepared for Confirmation, others who are lapsed communicants returning to Parish Communion, and some perhaps offering themselves to teach in the house Sunday school. In this parish seventy per cent of our children have to cross a main road to come to the parish church and the parish hall, and for this reason amongst others we are trying to build up nursery classes all over the parish, particularly on the Halton Moor Estate (6,000 population), entirely through the house-school. The class should not be very large—a good text for much of our education work would be 'The people are too many.' This contact with the home through the children and other contacts with adults through the homes is helping to give the congregation a sense of mission which as a congregation they have never had before.

The children's work is gradually being brought into the very centre of the Church's life and witness. As an example, at the annual meeting, 1953, the main report presented to the congregation was entitled, 'The Parish Church and the Church's Children.' The following should be taken as an indication of the approach of the Church towards the Church's children and not as a blue-print.

### Report on Children's Work

1. *Children's Council*

The organizing and co-ordinating body for children's work in the parish should be the children's council consisting of all leaders of children's organizations, Sunday school teachers, together with representatives of the Parochial Church Council and the congregation (including, of course, parents). The effective working of the council would help to bring about unity of aim and avoid the lapses of children which occur both from Sunday school and from organizations.

2. *The aim* of all the children's work is to prepare the children for Confirmation and for lives of faithful Church membership. Under this aim the support of the congregation is asked for:

(i) Holy Baptism, as at present administered quarterly: being the occasion for admission of new members into the Church and the point from which preparation for Confirmation starts.

(ii) Confirmation, as at present administered, with the Confirmation godparents sponsoring the newly confirmed into the full life of the Church.

(iii) Home meetings and house celebrations, especially as they are one of the chief ways of making contact with homes and parents, many of whom are, in fact, lapsed communicants.

3. There are four chief ways of fulfilling the aim of all the children's work:

(i) Children's worship: At the 9.30 Parish Communion with parents from infancy (nursery class in hall); or, where parents are not regular, at 9.30 after the age of about nine, with Sunday school teachers or leaders of organizations, with a worshipping family, or with other adult members of the congregation.

At special services for parents and children—Mothering Sunday, missionary week-end, and so on.

At the two Baptism services each year held in the afternoon.

On the greater weekday festivals—Christmas, Ash Wednesday, Ascension Day, Patronal Festival.

(ii) Sunday schools as at present organized—chief needs are for teachers for the over eleven and under four age groups.

(iii) Organizations—as at present—with full co-operation of the leaders in the whole plan for the children.

(iv) In children's home meetings from time to time and, where fitting, in groups meeting in a home (your home!).

4. Confirmation classes are but the culmination of the whole training with special instruction needed for the sacraments and special individual help.

Children would be readily accepted for Confirmation when they come from a worshipping home at the age when they seem ready. Where parents are not regular worshippers the age would be studied more carefully; children should normally have been regular at Parish Communion. In all cases any under eleven have to be considered by the bishop as well as the parish clergy.

5. The Confirmation candidates with their parents should be invited together with those confirmed during the past five years to a social organized by or on behalf of the P.C.C. and other members of the congregation should be present.

The proper organization for the newly confirmed is the parish branch of the Anglican Young People's Association which should help the young people into the life of the Church.

There should be an effort to get all to become members of the electoral roll at eighteen, perhaps with a refresher course.

6. Religion in the home: we should encourage family prayers and Bible reading. Blessing of homes and children's corners. The priest should be called in in cases of sickness, for laying on of hands.

These methods are encouraged in various ways, notably by the work of the Mothers' Union and the Young Wives' Group. There is a noticeable lack of opportunity to reach fathers, or fathers and mothers together, apart from home meetings and the house-church: therefore, these are the most important means of building up the Christian frontier and helping the congregation to be a missionary community.

The Convocation reports, *Baptism To-day*, *Confirmation To-day*, and other contemporary statements are all affirming the truth that Christian initiation includes Baptism, Confirmation, and Communion. They are all of a piece. Some would say that theologically we cannot separate the initiatory rites in time: most would say that they can be separated in time, but never in intention. At a clergy gathering recently a church dignitary claimed that of all the pastoral work of the clergy the least rewarding was the preparation and follow-up of Baptism. Much of the short-term evidence at Halton would support this, but in the long run nothing else we tackle will be effectively done unless we start with our attitude towards membership. Baptism declares man's need to live by grace in a fallen world, but it cannot properly do this unless the initiatory rites are held together. Here is the basis for pastoral reform. Link Baptism and Confirmation and Communion with marriage. Link Baptism, Confirmation, and Communion with burial, just as Baptism, Confirmation, and Communion are linked with ordination. Here is the way of restoring and building up the priesthood of the whole Church. If the centre of the ordination service and the centre of the ordained priest's life is the Communion service, then it also should be the centre of the life of the whole priestly body. The wrong ideas of the ordained ministry and its office and function are largely due to a wrong conception of the Church, a wrong conception of church membership. The Church is a priestly Church by Baptism. The apostolic succession is not just through bishops, the special ministers of the succession: the succession is basically through the whole Body which has died with Christ and risen with Him. Here is the new creation, the new ministerial church, the new priestly body.

If we are to deal rightly with membership, it is of the utmost importance that we administer the sacraments so that the initiatory rites are seen as great acts of the Church. Large numbers of people who have been baptized in the Church of England have never seen a Communion service.

Arising from the initiatory rites, what ought we now to do about godparents? The foreword to the draft body of canons says, 'We have followed in the tradition of the Church of England "the mean between the two extremes of too much stiffness in refusing and of too much easiness in admitting."' Canon 29 in the old canons forbids any one to be admitted godparents before they have received Communion. The new Canon 31, 'Of Sponsors,' says that 'for every child that is to be baptized there shall be at least one godparent of the same sex, who shall have been confirmed and who shall not be the child's parent.' Here we have the Church realizing that it is impossible to insist on three communicant godparents; it insists that one of the godparents should be a full member of the Church, while leaving the door open for one or even both of the parents to act as godparents. The *follow-up* of Baptism lies not with the godparents but with the parents. The difficulty in enforcing any canon or rubric about communicant sponsors for Baptism or Confirmation is that membership and worship, Baptism and Communion, have been separated in so many cases. As long as this divorce continues it will be almost impossible to develop the right sort of attitude towards sponsorship. What we need is not so much new canons, but a renewal of the Church.

We need so to present the services in church that people see the need to live by grace and so to act as a fellowship inside and outside the church building that we draw the lapsed baptized into that vital relationship with God through Jesus Christ which finds its focal point in the breaking of the bread. He was known two thousand years ago in the breaking of the bread.

We can talk for a very long time about the relationship between Baptism, Confirmation, and Communion, but most people need to see them together before they see the connection. It is the same in the instruction that has to be given as an essential part of the link between Baptism and Communion. Canon 34, 'Of Catechizing,' states:

1. Every minister shall take care that the children and young people within his cure are instructed in the doctrine, sacraments, and discipline of Christ, as the Lord has commanded and as they are received and set forth in the Church of England; and to this end he, or some godly and competent persons appointed by him, shall every Sunday diligently instruct and teach them in the same.

All parents and guardians shall cause their children to come to such instruction at the time and place appointed.

The difficulty is that where there is no sense of the Church as the eucharistic fellowship, there is very little background on which to base this instruction.

In Canon 35:

2. When the bishop shall assign any time for the performance of that part of his duty, every minister that has a cure of souls shall remind his people that all persons who have been baptized and are come to a competent age, and have not been confirmed, are to be brought to the bishop for Confirmation, and to all such as desire to be confirmed at that time he shall carefully teach the Christian faith as set forth in the Church Catechism and in the Book of Common Prayer.

3. The minister shall present none to the bishop but such as can say the Creed, the Lord's Prayer, and the Ten Commandments and can render an account of their faith according to the said Catechism.

After a certain amount of instruction many of the people who come forward for Confirmation can be taught to understand something of the meaning of the Christian faith as set forth in the Church Catechism and will be able to say the Creed, Lord's Prayer, and the Ten Commandments. But what they do not understand is the need to live by grace: what they do not understand is their place in the eucharistic fellowship. Once we see that Confirmation instruction begins at the font we see that the preparation must include everything over the whole period from Baptism to Confirmation itself.

The Bishop of Knaresborough has stressed the need for a new attitude towards preparation for Confirmation in his 'Memorandum on the proposal to substitute the name "Confirmation School" for "Sunday School."' Whether we change the name or not is secondary, but a revolution in the way a congregation looks at Sunday school and Confirmation is essential.

Some years ago, Canon Browne-Wilkinson suggested that the use of the term 'Confirmation school' for those children (Eleven plus) who were above the age for Junior School (7–11) and were therefore in the immediately pre-Confirmation age group.

The proposal of this Memorandum is that the name 'Confirmation school' should be taken further back and made the basic title for all the Church's children's instruction in place of the name 'Sunday school.'

1. In any case, the name 'Sunday school' has long ceased to represent the original intention of the founders of Sunday schools. They were designed to give not merely religious instruction, but the only elementary education then offered to masses of the poorest children, provided on Sundays as the only day available. The Church of England has for a number of reasons been uneasy with the title for some time and in many parishes other names have been tried in its place. In the highest quarters the term Voluntary Religious Education has been officially substituted for it, but this is too clumsy for use at the parochial level. The proposal is therefore to use the term 'Confirmation school' for the whole of our parochial work of instruction of children.

2. The basis of our children's work in the parishes is, I submit, the closing directions in the Baptismal Office in the Prayer Book, viz.: that the newly baptized are to be brought to the bishop to be *confirmed* and instructed in the Creed, etc., and catechism to that end. If this were taken *from the start* as the avowed aim and purpose of all our children's instruction (on Sundays or weekdays) it would greatly help and the name 'Confirmation school' rather than 'Sunday school' would bring the point into constant prominence. It would help—

G

(i) The children: 'This is directed towards the completion of what happened at your Baptism: not just learning this and that, but preparing you for the next stage in membership in the family of God.'

(ii) Their parents (careless or otherwise): 'Our school is intended to help *you* in the implementing of your baptismal undertakings, not just, vaguely, to give "religious" instruction.'

(iii) The teachers: Sunday school teachers are not infrequently little related to the communicant life of the parish.

(iv) The congregation, so far as they take any interest, such as of course they should, in the 'younger end' of the family of God in their parish. They too would be encouraged by the use of such a name to see the place of children's instruction in the parish policy.

(v) Even bishops! When one goes to visit a parish the question 'How is your Sunday school going?' may receive an answer merely in the number of children. 'How is your Confirmation school going?' would obviously require an answer on the lines of 'How far is it fulfilling its declared purpose of leading your baptized children into full membership of the Church?' (For, of course, Confirmation is not an end in itself, but is the gateway to Communion and to going forth 'into the world to serve God faithfully in the fellowship of His Church'). (1928 Baptism Service).

It would, in fact, throw the emphasis of our children's work on membership, and that would be good also for all Church people.

3. Further, it would make plain to all concerned that our Church 'Sunday schools' are aiming at something different from those of other religious bodies. At best, Nonconformist Sunday schools are concerned with building their children into the adult life of the chapel, and we may rightly wish them well. They are doing, on their lines, just what we are trying to do. They don't practise Confirmation, and therefore our 'Confirmation schools' would be clearly distinguished from their plans for preparation for communicant membership in their denomination.

In this parish we asked ourselves whether Confirmation classes would not take a more central part in our church life if we decentralized them from the church building

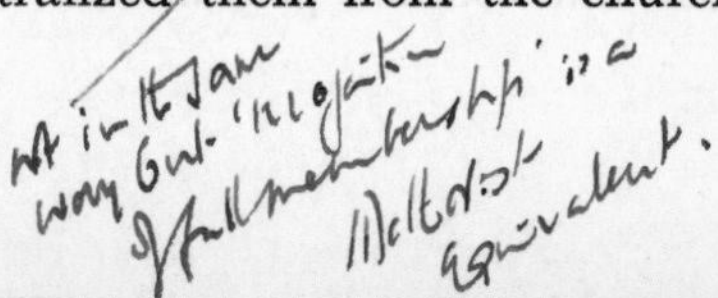

and hall into the homes. We thought that this would provide a real opportunity for the communicant members to meet the candidates from time to time and also that there would be a chance to make a steady and worthwhile link with the homes. This has, in fact, worked out, for since 1954 all the Confirmation classes have been taking place in homes, with occasional house celebrations as visual aids of the sacrament and of the communicant fellowship and of God's claim upon the homes and lives of His people. Adult as well as children's Confirmation classes met in houses. This meant that there were small fellowships meeting together regularly and meeting the larger church fellowship week by week at the Parish Communion. Each class had its own characteristics, its own experience and approach to things, so the instructions could be made much less general and vague: with a class meeting in a room, with the usual background of whistling kettles and barking dogs, there couldn't be less shyness or irrelevance or evasion of the issue: the Bible and the evening paper could be on the same table, and before the evening was out they would be in the same conversation too. Here the Church could again be a fellowship of learning, for as soon as possible during the evening the meeting would turn into a discussion instead of just an instruction and people would start to learn from each other. House Confirmation classes have not cut the candidates off from the fellowship of the Church: they have in fact helped them to get to know those who are already communicants, for on several occasions there have been celebrations of Communion at the classes and people have come to them to share in the Communion and meet the candidates. Nor have the candidates been cut off from each other: apart from meeting at the Parish Communion and organizations, the younger ones were together for a day at our diocesan retreat house, a day that has been in many ways the highlight of their whole preparation.

In Halton in 1954 we specially tried to bring the adults and young people together, using the whole of the church's organization—an Evensong conducted entirely by young people, a dance run by the youth council, ten house services conducted by young people, and eight home meetings to which young and old were invited. At the home meetings, especially, people did get to know each other. The youth Evensong and house services happened in the last week-end before the Confirmation, which was taken as a special week-end of preparation. When the bishop came on the Friday he started at the last stage of preparation by going round to a series of house celebrations in houses of candidates in the evening, and so they and the communicant members could meet him together as he visited the homes. We had several candidates who were elderly and unable to get to church, and some were bedridden: so on Saturday the bishop held Confirmations in four houses and at the house celebrations that followed immediately the bishop preached and the candidates shared in the Communion for the first time. For two elderly couples this day was what they had been looking forward to for thirty years and more: one of these couples had their daughter and her husband present with them; they were to be confirmed themselves on the Sunday, and they had brought their two children up to the house with them; the man's old employer was there, too, in the congregation, and so was the local city councillor. The milkman knocked on the door with a bill during the service; he was asked to come back later as the bishop was there, and when he asked, 'Is it that serious?' one thought of all these people and what God was doing in their midst and the answer was not hard to find!

It was serious, too, when at the public service of preparation on the Saturday night the bishop baptized four candidates; and immediately afterwards one of them, who would be working on the Sunday morning, came forward with his sponsor to be confirmed. Nothing could have shown more clearly how Baptism and Confirmation are linked and how they fit in with each other; and next morning at the Parish Communion we saw again how Confirmation and Communion are linked and how they fit in with each other: the bishop, robed as the celebrant of the Eucharist, at the chancel step confirmed the remaining candidates, about fifty in number; and the witnesses, who had been sitting behind the candidates, moved up with them and stood behind them as they knelt before the bishop. When he put his hands on the head of each candidate, and said 'Defend, O Lord, this thy child . . .' the witness, as is the custom in some places overseas, put his right hand on the right shoulder of the candidate. The bishop then moved up to the east side of the high altar to preside at the family meal of the people of God.

It was the meal of the whole family, the newly confirmed and those who had known Christ in Communion for many years. The witnesses came up with the newly confirmed; they sat beside them at the parish breakfast and were meant to have a special spiritual relationship with them within the fellowship of the church. There is no doubt that having Confirmation and Communion together demonstrates the unity of the initiatory rite. Now the whole organization of the Church must be brought into play to preserve, deepen, and extend that unity of young and old that is both made and symbolized at the altar: all our Baptism work, Confirmation work, Parish Communion, church organizations and services are to help us, as a Church and as individual members, to see our discipleship as the serious thing that it actually is, that together we may grow into maturity as inheritors of the kingdom of heaven.

The bishop's presence brings home another point. He is exercising his cure of souls. One of the things that comes out of the motto 'Let the Church be the Church' is the subsidiary one 'Let the bishop be the bishop.' If there are not enough bishops for them to go round celebrating at parish altars in their diocese then we ought to have more bishops, so that a bishop has more opportunity of acting as a bishop within each parish.

What is true of Confirmation is true of Baptism. The bishop should occasionally baptize at the parish font: then the people see more clearly the connection between Baptism, Confirmation, and Communion. At the present moment most Church people associate the bishop first and foremost with Confirmation. We must free the bishop so that he can exercise his pastoral function in the parish. The bishop ought to be freed so that he can come to the parish for a few days at a time. He ought to be able to go round and visit the sick folk. He ought to be able to meet the Parochial Church Council and the children's council and the Mothers' Union and the youth group. He ought to be able to baptize, confirm, and celebrate Communion, marry couples, take a funeral, visit the house-church, share in some of the difficult interviews that the vicar is trying to cope with at that time. He would be able to get alongside the situation in the parish by being there with priest and people—at a meal with the churchwarden, at a meal with the trade-union leader, or the secretary of the youth group, or the caretaker. He would be alongside in a way that the parish and its people would appreciate. Let the bishops enter their parishes, let the bishops help to build up the Church in the parish. There is a principle in this: it will build up our conception of the Church and help us to realize what it means to be an episcopal Church.

But when all this is done, it is obvious that the Church's teaching work has scarcely started. Abbé Michonneau puts the challenge in another way. He takes the Parable of the Lost Sheep and says that now there is one in the fold and ninety-nine out in the wilderness, and the Church spends most of its time mollycoddling the one in the fold and ignoring the ninety-nine in the wilderness! We must get on talking terms with those out of touch with the

Church, the majority of whom are just apathetic: they see no need to live by grace.

The place where we can meet where values still count is the home, the natural community which finds its prototype in the life of God the ever-blessed Trinity. The problem of the home is the world problem writ small and the world problem is the home problem writ large. The home is the training ground for the brotherhood of man under the fatherhood of God. The home is the place where community is to be realized and the battle against the world, the flesh, and the devil is to be waged.

Let us look at those who have been married in church. In the last ten years I have married over 800 couples, but only about half a dozen of them have had their marriage completed with the Communion service. Although one has done one's best to try and show to couples in meeting them beforehand their need to live by grace, the majority of them have no background of experience and do not and cannot be expected to understand. To them the Church and its sacraments are a thing apart.

This is what we have tried in Halton. During the second week in November, 1953, members of the congregation met in five houses for the breaking of the bread, and to discuss how we can help people to see the very close connection between marriage and the Communion; how could we help them to see that it is not sufficient merely to receive the initial act of grace in order to live out the implications of the marriage service? We discussed the tragedy of separating marriage from Communion. One of the things that came home to us at these meetings is that we ought to encourage couples to have the Communion service at a wedding whenever they are confirmed, and ask those who are not confirmed whether they are prepared to have a Communion service before or after their marriage. This helps some of them to be confirmed as part of their post-marriage instruction. The unconfirmed at a marriage service with Communion will be helped to see that the service is meant to take place in the context of the Communion service, which is intended to be the best way of helping the married couple to build up their home. If this is all true, obviously the bride's father, who presents the bride for marriage, and those who sign the register, usually the best man and one of the bridesmaids, ought to be communicants too, for they are presenting two members of the Church as bona fide members of the Church for holy marriage.

Normally a parish priest interviews couples before marriage. Many of us find it useful to offer pamphlets to these couples. One of the best of these I believe to be *The Threshold of Marriage*, a practical guide for all who intend to be married in church (revised in 1949).[1]

This pamphlet has had numerous editions and reprints and by July 1951 had reached its 380th thousand. I want to take a quotation from it to illustrate the difficulty of trying to lead most of our marriage couples to a vital relationship to Christ in the fellowship of His Church.

HOLY COMMUNION: The Prayer Book says that it is right that the newly married pair should receive Holy Communion together immediately after the marriage ceremony, or at the first opportunity after it.

Beware of magical and superstitious ideas. The Blessing given in the Marriage Service is not a supply of grace sufficient for a life-time. It represents a beginning and assumes that the couple will go on regularly using the means of grace and continually receiving divine help in their weekly worship and their daily private prayers.

Many married people make a point of coming to church and to Holy Communion on or near the anniversary of their wedding: after examining themselves to see how each has done his or her part, they renew before God the solemn vows which they took on the day they were married.

I'm sure that most clergy would feel that for the majority of the couples they interview the phrase 'continually

[1] Published for the Church of England Moral Welfare Council by the Church Information Board, 6*d*.

receiving divine help in their weekly worship and their daily private prayers' is a very far cry: most of us would also agree that while the Prayer Book is right about receiving the Holy Communion at the time of the marriage or soon after, it is impossible because bride and bridegroom are seldom both confirmed.

For twelve years I prepared couples for marriage in Halton and tried to stress the need for seeing marriage as an offering of two people to God and to each other, body, mind, and spirit: I tried to show the need for worship and prayer. Most of the 1,200 prepared during this time have come at least once to hear their banns read, but as far as I know not one who was not already regularly worshipping has come to worship after marriage either in this parish or in any other parish. None of them has asked to be confirmed. Are we just to accept this situation or are we to try and do something about it? I believe that either we must not marry people who are unconfirmed, or we must help them to want to be confirmed and regularly to participate in the weekly Communion.

On one occasion a couple came to put the banns in; an interview was arranged and they were asked to come and hear the banns, which they did; at the interview it was obvious that they had been very impressed to see so many people receiving Communion, so I asked the couple to consider having a celebration of Holy Communion in the girl's house. I explained quite simply that the marriage service was meant to take place in the context of the Communion service, that those being married in church were expected to receive Communion at the time of their marriage or at the first opportunity afterwards: the house celebration was to help them to take this seriously. At this moment one of our lay readers came with his wife to be churched, so I left the couple to think about it, and went off to the churching. When I returned they both said they were willing to have a house celebration. At the Parochial Church Council next night a member of the council said he went down to Leeds on the tram every morning with the girl; after she had been to put in the banns she had told this member that she had been asked to come to church to hear the banns, and she couldn't for the life of her see why; anyway, after she had attended the Parish Communion and heard the banns, she was obviously impressed; two weeks before the whole idea had seemed pointless, but now she was willing to have a house celebration. The house celebration took place during a home meeting with various relations present, including the bride's mother and father. The Communion service took place around that family table with the regular worshippers taking Communion and those of the household not being able to. I don't know what may happen as a result of this house celebration, but two of the five people were at Parish Communion the following Sunday.

This was just one of nine home meetings and house celebrations that we held during the fourth week in that November in houses of people who have been married in church but who are mostly unconfirmed; only one of the eighteen people is a regular communicant. I think it is important to realize that this situation is mainly not the fault of the people themselves: but the question of marriage shows up the divorce of the two communities, the congregation and the parish, more than almost anything else. Whatever we may say about what we are doing, it is quite certain that this second lot of home meetings would not have taken place if we hadn't started to build up the church out in the homes of the congregation. One of the couples has already offered for Confirmation, and I am sure that none of them will be unaffected by taking part in the breaking of bread in their own homes. All over the parish there are homes where the truth of God is needed, where the Church must show the fullness of Christian membership: so not merely the clergy, but the whole church goes out, to find its members, to heal the division between Baptism and Communion, between the congregation and the parish, to bring Christ *home* to His people.

## CHAPTER VIII

# *TRAINING THE CONGREGATION*

HOW do you get people to do this sort of thing? Does it somehow come easily to the people of Halton? No.[1] We, like most people, find it difficult to visit and also to witness personally for Christ. In the Church as a whole much exhortation is given about the responsibility of the Church to witness, but not much direction as to how it is to be done. Here at Halton the outgoing of the Church has come in part through the parish meeting. This has led to the house-church, the house Communion, the house service, the house Sunday school, the house Confirmation class. All these have given opportunities for the layman to be the Church, to say what Christ means to him, to share in Bible study, to share in discussing the faith in relationship to science, psychology, and economics, to meet visitors from other parishes, to meet members of other denominations, to discuss the parish policy about children's work, or old people's welfare, etc.

The Church is called to be a fellowship of learners. The Church is to provide the environment in which the education of souls is to take place. Canon J. R. Lumb in his book, *The Education of Souls*, reminds us 'that the Holy Spirit cannot teach the souls of non-worshipping children' and

you cannot teach non-worshipping adults to grow in grace and truth. Souls left much at the point where the last Confirmation class finished are at the mercy of many spiritual perils. The layman who cannot easily think of his Church except in the terms of what he calls 'finance' is really suffering from the spiritual starvation of a discontinued education.

The people who get tired and fall away because they 'have

[1] The parish is a very mixed one with private and council houses.

heard it all,' and equally those who are suspicious of anything that sounds new, are alike victims of the static view of grace and truth. Indeed, our whole Church life is like a pool. So easily the green film may form over its waters, which can be kept sweet only if the pool is continually made alive by running water. To many a weary priest, who pleads that he needs a change, and to many a Parochial Church Council which believes that it needs a new incumbent, the true pastoral answer would often be 'No; you need rather a united experiment in adult education.'[1]

I believe that the house-church is *the* way in which we are going to train adults to be the Church. There is probably still quite a lot of unsuspected faith and Christian experience among English people to-day: the trouble is they won't talk about it. Most sermons and most talks cut very little ice because the listener is not expected to say anything about them or pass on messages and so he doesn't listen as if he was going to. The parish meeting helps people to teach themselves what they know, but even in the parish meeting the majority will be silent because of the numbers, even if they are split up for group discussion. It is in the house that the real elementary training can start, training leaders by leading; in the house people are less likely than anywhere else to feel foolish and afraid of saying the wrong thing: and the experience of working in home meetings equips people to take on other jobs. For instance, all our house services on Sunday evenings—ten a month in the homes of people who cannot get to church—are taken by lay people, who preach and lead the prayers and read the Bible, etc. When we first planned them we asked one of the people whether he would take a service, and he agreed. But he added, 'Six months ago I should have said, "Not on your life!"' Why the change? Because in those six months he had taken part in the house-church, he had been persuaded to lead a home meeting (which he found after all he could do very well), and so he found himself

[1] Op. cit., p. 146.

prepared to preach at a service. The informal, friendly, and, above all, small meeting in the home compels people to get this practice in thinking and talking about the things of God.

Archbishop Temple once said that the greatest thing he envied in the Church of Scotland was its system of ruling elders: as the training of leaders developed in the house-church we have seen the need to have regular leaders in charge of the house-church in their particular areas and they take, under the parish priest, positions something like those of the Presbyterian elders. As different churches we may learn from each other in this way. For example, some members of the Iona community now feel that for them the way forward at the parish level is in the house-church. Perhaps this may lead to a restoration of a permanent diaconate. The meeting of the elders supplies a similar need to the Methodist leaders' meeting.[1]

Church people often forget the way their Church and religion appear to the outsider: our impact is often not as great as it might be because we answer the questions we *think* the outsider should ask and not the ones he does ask. In Halton there is no excuse for this happening, for in the extensive house-church, Church people take the Church into the homes of outsiders. These meetings have no set subject, for we are there to get to understand the outsider, to present the Church to him, and to see together how the Gospel answers his special needs and problems. Church people (including the clergy) learn as much as any one from these meetings. In these homes of outsiders we are being trained to see the present work of Christ among us, for whether many people are there or few, whether we are good arguers or bad, the central fact of the meeting is Christ's presence with us; not our

[1] In 1956 we have divided the parish into six areas, and each of these areas now has a permanent leader or warden; he normally leads the monthly intensive house-church, and with the help of street wardens he keeps the church in touch with the parish and the parish in touch with the church. These area wardens were commissioned by the bishop when he came for Confirmation.

attempts but God's success, not our ideas but God's action. When these meetings include celebrations of Holy Communion they can never become just gossip shops or just ecclesiastical publicity because the central act depends not on our cleverness but on God's power, God's promise, God's humility, God's action; and that sums up and sanctifies whatever else happens at the meeting.[1]

Here we are being trained to see the power of God and the availability of God and the relevance of God to any person or situation. And let no one think that because the Communion is in the evening, in a house, with a fire, with tea and refreshments afterwards, it is therefore cheap and easy compared to Communion at 7 a.m. in a cold church. No! Communion out on the frontier in enemy territory, where we see what a caricature of Christ we are, where we see what a huge missionary task is before us, where we see the weakness of Christ and the strength of the devil, Communion in that setting is as costing as in any circumstances we are likely to find in England to-day. Preparation for Communion *is* important and to receive Communion fasting is a laudable custom, but the preparation of charity is more important and to give up a whole evening and walk a mile to the house of a stranger to show him something of the meaning of the Church and the meaning of Communion is an example of the preparation of charity.

It is through this deepening of our corporate worship and the widening of our concern for those outside that we have felt the inadequacy of the way we look at the ministry. One reason for the weakness of the Church of England has been the false distinction between clergy and laity. Often still the clergy alone are thought of as the 'Church.' But it is the baptized laity who are the 'people of God.'

[1] It was just this sense of God-givenness that a Methodist minister, now working in the Church of South India, felt to be missing from the class meeting; after attending the house-church he said that the class meeting needed the Communion for it to be what it should be.

The clergy are a ministry of the laity who have been summoned to fulfil certain functions in the Church. The forward movement of Christian revolution, the work of evangelism, the Christianization of society—this is the vocation of Christian laymen whose whole business of living brings them into contact with all sorts and conditions of men. The laity can be an influence permeating society as the clergy never can. It is the task of bishops and priests to teach true doctrines. It is for the great body of lay Christians to go out and put these principles into practice in home, in local government, in business and industry, in education, and in all the relationships which make up human society. The religious revivals associated with the names of St. Anthony, St. Benedict, St. Francis, John Wesley, have been almost entirely lay movements.

In order to train himself the Christian needs to understand the Christian doctrines which are enshrined in the Church's liturgy. When he knows what the Christian faith is, he must hammer out the meaning of that faith in terms of daily life and work and the needs of the society in which he lives and works. Individual reading and thinking is essential. But individual study needs to be checked and broadened by study and discussion with other Christians, and it is in the regular meetings of Christians in each other's houses that this mutual training becomes most pertinent and personal. But this training need not be practised only in the house-church; the trained Christian must take the Church out beyond the parish boundaries.

It is essential that a Christian in an office or factory should meet other Christians in that place, both for their own mutual encouragement and to forward Christ's work. What they do when they do meet will depend on the particular circumstances. It may be they will spend much of the time simply in being alongside those for whom the Church is an anachronism, slowly breaking down the large but familiar barriers of prejudice, showing their belief that the formation of the new society has been part of God's hand in history. It is certainly part of the parish's job to train people to see this mission, to train people to be missionaries in modern society. And the parish must provide an environment into which a convert can be brought, where he would find a fellowship that is genuinely concerned about the consecration of modern developments in society, where he would find a quality of life unknown elsewhere. The Church in the parish must provide half-way houses and quarter-way houses to the parish church and mustn't be in a hurry to push people into the parish church. In fact, it could be said that one of the aims of the extensive house-church is to keep people out of the parish church because they are not yet ready for it, nor in many cases are the people in the parish church ready to receive them! If these people are not to go to the parish church where are they to go? We say, to the house-church. On the home front we have learned to testify to the sort of things that Canon E. R. Wickham and others are doing on the industrial front.

It is the basic aim of the industrial mission to discover, equip, and bring together men who will go through the hard discipline of studying Christianity in a new kind of way and to work out its possible bearing on the many problems and strains of industry and the larger industrial society in which modern men have to live.[1]

There is also a considerable concern in the Church to help us to see what our individual responsibility for the corporate life and witness of the Church is. For instance, here is Resolution 37 of the 1945 Lambeth Conference:

The Conference urges all Church people to look upon their membership of Christ in the Church as the central fact in their lives. They should regard themselves as individually sharing responsibility for the corporate life and witness of the Church in the places where they live. They should discharge this responsibility and give a distinctive witness:

[1] *Christian News Letter*, January, 1955. Canon E. R. Wickham.

(*a*) by the regularity of their attendance at public worship and especially at the Holy Communion;

(*b*) by the practice of private prayer, Bible reading, and self-discipline;

(*c*) by bringing the teaching and example of Christ into their everyday lives;

(*d*) by the boldness of their spoken witness to their faith in Christ;

(*e*) by personal service to Church and community;

(*f*) by the offering of money, according to their means, for the support of the work of the Church at home and overseas.

Thus there will be in every locality a living centre of Christian faith, witness, and fellowship.

In a Church Assembly report we are reminded that

it is now commonly forgotten that the Church has from the first imposed on her members a certain common discipline, by means of which they are bound together in a common loyalty and obedience and built up into a common life of the Body of Christ.

It is this need for common loyalty that is so much needed in our Church life.

Further light has been thrown on the need for a Rule of Life for members in the short guide to *Duties of Church Membership* put out by the two archbishops.

It is because of this need for loyalty to Christ and the Church and because of the need for this to be brought out in a practical way that a group of clergy in Leeds started to meet together at Ember seasons to report on the observance of a common rule.[1]

For many years here I have felt the need for some sort of group keeping a common rule in the parish, but I have hesitated because of the danger of its becoming a spiritual clique. It is obvious that the Parochial Church Council and the parish meeting ought to be such a group. It is equally obvious that it is difficult for them to be so.

For eighteen months a group of about thirty people

[1] Groups like this have been springing up all over the country.

met here at quarterly intervals, not under a rule, but simply to consider whether we were being called to one. We had as the basis of our thinking a detailed rule of eighteen clauses, concerning charity, loyalty to each other, prayer, and participation in the various activities of the Church inside and outside the church building. During our eighteen months of trying to work out our obedience in this matter we have come to see that it is probably not this sort of rule that is needed: so in August, 1955, we arranged a meeting to discuss the formation of a group under a new rule, and the following notice appeared in the parish magazine for that month:

If the work of Christ in His Body the Church in this place is to be carried forward in the parish as a whole, we need a group to which any one can come, but which is committed to God according to a special rule. Such as:

1. To pray daily at home or in the parish church according to a personal rule.
2. To take the Bible seriously each day.
3. To use the sacraments according to rule.
4. To let Christ have a say about our home, work, leisure, friendships.
5. To exercise charity to others, especially towards those with whom we don't agree or whom we find it difficult to like.
6. To exercise concern for the policy in this place.

Pray and pray about this—Baptism, Parish Communion, house-church, Ecumenism, political obedience, all mean more now. In all ages God has used special groups to do certain things for Him. I believe we need a special group now in Halton to work and pray with the clergy.

That was the notice in the magazine. But we in Halton are not trying to tell the Holy Spirit His job, nor have we elaborated any doctrine of the infallibility of the vicar! In fact, by the end of that meeting there was a common mind, to the effect that we should have no such group, but that the whole congregation should undertake its life with a new and deliberate discipline.

These rules will never be kept by the bulk of the Church people unless the life of fellowship in the parish is built up on that loyalty to God and loyalty to each other which helps the people to see the need for a rule. Too many of the rules of the Church have failed because Christians have seen their call to the Christian life as purely an individual one. It is as the Christian more and more falls in love with the beloved community that the extent of the call to charity and service are seen.[1]

It has been insisted that the renewal in the Church to-day is a theological revival, and that means essentially a biblical revival. People must be given the opportunity to learn as the pioneer theologians have learned, from the Bible. We have found that we must meet to study the Word of God regularly, to learn together to be a preaching church. It was said at the Minneapolis Conference that no other communion uses the Bible in its services as much as the Anglicans; none the less, it has been largely due to meeting with Christians of other traditions that we have been led as Anglicans to try to break the Word together as seriously as we break bread together. We have had Bible study in various forms; sometimes in the hall, like a parish meeting; more recently we have been holding it in church, before Evensong on Sunday, with a final summary in the sermon, after Evensong instead of the sermon, or during Evensong after the second lesson, in the place appointed for catechizing; and we have met regularly in homes to study Bible-Reading Fellowship notes together. Here, too, is a great oppor-

[1] This call to work in community is now to be answered in Halton not by a group under a rule, but by a number of people working together in teams. In September 1956 we are having a Campaign (not a 'mission,' because the mission of the Church is on all the time); about forty students from Cambridge will be with us for a fortnight; in the first week we plan to have ten extensive house-churches each evening, and each of these will be taken by a team of about four people who will stay together and plan the follow-up of each meeting in the following week and in the future; and as we have already mentioned, the house Evensong will be taken by a series of teams, each one consisting of four to six people, who will be a good mixture of folk from the congregation: they will divide the various parts of the service between them.

tunity for Christians of different traditions to get to know and understand each other, to reveal to each other the truths and interpretations that have shaped their particular expression of Christian obedience. As we come together to study the Bible we should feel encouraged to use it more seriously in private.

The question is: How?

One way is the method of 'corporate mental action,' worked out for the Anglican Young People's Association and described in full in Volume 1 of *Unto a Full Grown Man*, by S. H. Evans and E. W. Southcott (National Society and S.P.C.K.). This is a method of study for groups coming together to work out their Christian discipleship in terms of worship, work, fellowship, and edification; it is an attempt to adopt and redefine the traditional type of Bible study. At Halton the Anglican Young People's Association has been using this method regularly. Each session is divided into five parts: Prepare, some minutes of spoken and silent prayer; Picture, the Bible reading and a short instruction on it; Ponder, general discussion on selected questions designed to help the members to relate what they have heard to their daily life; Pray, a short meditation, suitable intercessions, and acts of adoration; Promise, a time for offering resolutions for action.

'This is all very well, but where does God come into it all?' Obviously He comes in everywhere, on every page, in every meeting. 'Yes, but it's very easy to fit God in here and there, just to give tone to it all, as it were, to call on the Blessed Trinity to give your work a reassuring flavour of the New Testament. Is it all laid on as if we could get by without God?' As we have said, we do believe that this work of the Church, the work of the Church across the world and the work of the Church in Halton, is the work of the Holy Spirit; but it cannot be all according to His will if each individual is not keeping himself consciously in touch and receiving orders. We have to train each other to pray. Christians have to be recalled to the devotional life because each of us has to be won to the necessity of prayer. There are very few people who do not have to move from the early stage of thinking that 'conduct is of supreme importance and prayer helps it' to the maturer stage of admitting in practice that 'prayer is of supreme importance and conduct tests it,' as William Temple taught.

This recall to the devotional life inevitably involves discipline; part of this discipline comes in the daily house celebration, when there is always a time for people to bring in their own prayers, thanksgivings, and confessions, either out loud or in the silence: the house celebration stirs our prayer into our daily life, and our daily life into our prayer. Part of this discipline is regular daily prayer with the Scriptures, as we are determined to let God show us Himself at work. We believe that we can still be 'together' though we may be separated in time and place, so we try to let God reveal Himself to us 'together' as we each read the same piece of the Bible day by day; therefore we run just one series of the Bible-Reading Fellowship notes in the parish.

But many people feel the need for help and guidance that is fuller than that given by the Bible-Reading Fellowship. Some feel the need, and probably many more half-feel the need, to advance into mental prayer of a more guided and thoughtful kind; but it is difficult to recommend them to try the classical methods that have come down to us, for these have been shaped by environment and thought-forms and experiences so different from our own. Even if an ordinary layman succeeded in adjusting himself so that he could use the methods of the masters naturally, he would run a considerable risk of failing to relate his meditation, with its specialized mental processes, to his ordinary life in the twentieth-century shop or office. Yet there is still the need for mental prayer, and in principle the prayer of all Christians is the same. We have much to value and use in our inheritance from those who have opened their minds to

God in the past. The individual's mental prayer should be seen as part of the prayer of the whole Church, and therefore it can with advantage follow the pattern of corporate prayer. It can link itself up consciously with the prayers of the whole Church by falling back on the great choruses of the liturgy as a kind of daily refrain, discovering new truth, new relevance, new applications of them in their richness: they are the voice of Christian experience; they express the need that our prayer has told us of, and the glory that it has shown; they foretell possessions for which we can find no words, and confess deficiencies that we scarcely see.

This chapter closes with an example of how these methods can be worked out in practice for personal prayer and meditation. I am sure that there is a need for a way of prayer which is more related to everyday life than are the traditional methods of meditation. Here is one day out of a proposed book of prayers for the days of the Christian Year.

'If we are to follow Christ, it must be in our common way of spending every day.'[1]

PREPARE. Spend several minutes realizing the presence of God and in talking and listening to Him.

PICTURE. 'Go ye therefore, and teach all nations, baptizing them in the Name of the Father, and of the Son, and of the Holy Ghost' (*St. Matt.* xxviii. 19). St. Matthew xxviii. 16–20.

PONDER. Each Christian is to proclaim God's message by his words and by his actions—'in Jerusalem,' in his own home and among his own friends; 'in all Judaea,' in his own district as worker and citizen; 'in Samaria,' among strangers and people whom he doesn't like; 'and unto the uttermost parts of the earth,' in India and China and the South Seas; 'Go . . .' These are our marching orders and a Christian who is not a missionary is not a Christian

[1] W. Law, *Serious Call.*

at all. The Christian goes in prayer and in action, for prayer is action. To join the Church in prayer is to join the Church in work. It means bringing all the work of the Church, bit by bit, and placing it at the foot of the Cross. It means adoring Christ and leaving the results to Him. God wants to heal all men everywhere, to make them whole and to make them holy. He uses us in the barrack-room, in the works lunch hour, in our friendships, through reading, through service, through prayer. He wants to remake us and remould us according to His plan, and to prepare us for eternal life with God.

Who comes? Jesus.

How does He come? Quietly in the ordinary life of man.

Why does He come? To restore man to his high calling.

PRAY. To Christ on the Cross.

Glory be to God on high, and may Thy *Faith* be with all men that they may recognize Christ as God speaking.

*Confess*. O Lamb of God, that takest away the sins of the world, grant us Thy *Faith*.

Let us give thanks unto our Lord God.

It is meet and right so to do.

Therefore with angels and archangels, and with all the company of heaven, we laud and magnify Thy glorious Name; evermore praising Thee, and saying: Holy, holy, holy, Lord God of hosts, heaven and earth are full of Thy *Faith*; glory be to Thee, O Lord, Most High.

PROMISE. To make an act of love—'O my God, I do love Thee. O my God, I want to love Thee more and more for ever and ever. Amen.'

Thought for to-day:

'If I forget Thee this day, Lord, do not forget me.'

Worship, meeting, discipline, prayer: by all these means, God is training the congregation.

CHAPTER IX

# HEAL THE SICK

ARE you well? If you haven't got a cold, and haven't broken your leg, and haven't got lumbago, you answer, 'I'm fine, thanks.' If you replied, 'My body is well, but I've got a pain in my mind and my soul's in a shocking state,' most people would think you were a bit eccentric. Partly because the Church had neglected the ministry of healing and partly because the Church had taught that sickness and disease was a visitation from God, medicine has developed very largely apart from Christian teaching. There are so many bodily ills and diseases and naturally the concentration has been on the cure of these. After the first concentration on physical healing the relationship of mind and body was rediscovered, sometimes by medical men and sometimes by spiritualists and Christian Scientists. The Christian Church came rather late in the field, but during the last twenty-five years there has been a considerable number of individuals, together with organizations like the Guild of Health and the Guild of St. Raphael, who have brought the challenge of healing to the Christian Church.

The tendency has been to stick to water-tight compartments: often when Christians discovered this healing work they described it as divine healing or spiritual healing. There may be some truth in these adjectives, but they are misleading to a Christian doctor, a Christian psychiatrist, and also to a Christian patient, to say nothing of their being misleading to those who do not express any belief in Christianity.

Healing work has its specialists, but healing and health must be looked on as a whole. The word 'health' itself needs to be brought out of its narrow connotation.

From the Anglo-Saxon word *hale* come the words whole, healthy, holy. We are all called to be whole, healthy, holy; we are all to grow unto the full-grown man. 'If there is a thorn in the foot, the whole body must stoop down to pick it up'; this in itself applies most wonderfully to the team work in Christian healing. Doctors, nurses, psychiatrists, priests, probation officers, health visitors, friends, relations, members of the congregation, all can help in the stooping down. There is a need to help congregations to build themselves up into a healing fellowship, a fellowship in which Christ acts in His Church to-day, in which Christ stretches forth His hand to heal. The healing fellowship will grow as the Church is faithful to her Lord, as the Church becomes the Church.

A few years ago a young Halton man left the forces with T.B. He was healed, but had a relapse; he was receiving Communion each week, but not making much progress. About that time there was a series of youth home meetings, and at one of these there was a request that they should be given something to do. It was suggested that they might turn out in force on the next Thursday morning at 6.30 a.m. at this man's house. It was the most thrilling experience to celebrate Holy Communion in the presence of sixteen young people gathered round the bed. He is now completely restored to health and is very happily married. We believe his restoration began that morning.

At a parish meeting once we were just finishing when a man of fifty got up and said that he would like to have a word. He gave a little testimony which ran something like this. A year ago he had been an incurable epileptic and was out of work. About that time his wife went to a home meeting. She came home so enthusiastic that he went to the next one. Gradually, bit by bit, he came into the worshipping community. He started Confirmation classes, had the laying on of hands, was prepared for Confirmation, Communion, and confession. He had been worshipping then for over six months (it is now over three years). He was completely cured, and he wanted to say thank you to the house-church and the parish church. Other illustrations could be given, and I am quite convinced that as the Church becomes more and more the Church, the Body of Christ, then in it and through it the power of Christ will heal.

The whole human race has fallen. That fall has affected every part of every being. Every part of us is related to every other part, and every one is related to every one else. We do not know what the answer is to all the problems of life, nor do we understand the full implications of sin, suffering, and disease. What we do know is that Christ came into the sin-laden disease-infested world, and He suffered as no one else has suffered. The meaning of this suffering was redemption. Redemption means salvation, and salvation means new creation, and new creation means re-creation of body, mind, and soul. The special sign of Christ's special presence with us, the present proof of His Resurrection and heavenly intercession for us, is the Communion service, and Communion is to preserve our bodies and souls into everlasting life. We must look at the doctrine of redemption.

In Genesis we are told that God looked at everything and beheld that it was good. Bishop Neville Talbot wrote that the truest thing about man was not that he is a sinner, but that he is made in the image of God, and however marred or disfigured it may be the image is still there. Christ came to restore that image in all men, to make men whole. The Church which is His Body is called to continue Christ's saving work, and part of that saving work is to heal the sick. The Church is called to fight sickness and disease as well as sin, wherever it finds them. It may well be that in a fallen world sin and disease will remain till the final consummation of all things, but that does not mean the Church is not called to use every possible means to fight them.

The call to healing is first and foremost a call to prayer.

If the Church has neglected the ministry of healing for a thousand years it won't be restored in five minutes. Healing groups, praying for the sick in mind, body, and soul, are needed, but the healing work of the Church is to be seen increasingly as the vocation of the whole worshipping congregation.

It may be that this is the way in which a revival of healing is to take place. The people that are prayed for at worship, Sunday by Sunday, and day by day, are the concern of the whole Christian congregation. Increasingly, the whole congregation must realize its vocation to offer up people in the setting of corporate worship to God the Father, through Jesus Christ in the power of the Spirit. The Eucharist is obviously the appropriate place for this to be done, and the element of thanksgiving, which is one of the key notes of the Communion service, is one of the key notes of the interceding eucharistic fellowship. The congregation needs to learn to return thanks as well as to pray for the sick. One of the things that has come out of the house-church has been that people are encouraged to pray for those who are ill, and to return thanks for those who have recovered. At the house celebration before the Prayer for the Church Militant there is always a time for informal prayer.

The priest and certain lay folk may have a special vocation to visit the sick and lay hands on them, but the priest and visitors should all have a sense that they are acting on behalf of the congregation both in visiting and in laying on of hands.

This experience of informal prayer in houses, in which we have learned much from our Free Church friends, has led us to have monthly prayer meetings in church: these happen during the Parish Communion on the second Wednesday of the month. The Wednesday night programme is:

1st Wednesday. Parish Communion and Parochial Church Council.

2nd Wednesday. Parish Communion and Healing Service.

3rd Wednesday. Parish Communion and parish meeting with the Parochial Church Council.

4th Wednesday. Parish Communion and parish meeting with the missionary committee, the children's council, and the youth council, in rotation.

On the second Wednesday we have a fifteen-minute period of prayer before the Prayer for the Church, which sums up all our intercessions for the world, the Church, and individuals. At 'Draw near with faith' those desiring the laying on of hands gather round our nave altar and the congregation gathers round them: then those near help the priest with the laying on of hands. Christ stretches forth His hand to heal in the midst of the eucharistic Church. Then follows, 'Lift up your hearts.'

Eight years ago we had a group which used to meet regularly for prayer and the laying on of hands or anointing. This new prayer meeting may become a special time when people can be given the particular healing sacraments. The old group has now spread beyond Halton and has become the Leeds Fellowship of Healing and Prayer; it has become a most valuable meeting place for all kinds of Christians who are concerned with Christ's healing work. In the coming year it is joining with the Leeds Council of Churches in running a series of studies on anxiety—anxiety in the individual, anxiety in the family, in society, in international affairs, and so on; the leaders of the study will include priests and ministers, physicians and psychiatrists, a probation officer and our M.P. This is all part of the Church's attempt to show what healing Christians have to bring to this half-destroyed world.

As people see more and more that if they can't go to the church building the Church must come to them, as the people see more and more that if they can't come to the church building for Communion the Communion ought to be brought to them, the right approach should be taken to sickness and death. Some folks still think that if the parson comes some one must be dying. And if the parson brings the Communion the patient is as good as dead! The sick Communion household can be a real centre of Church life. Some of the Church's ministry to the sick, such as confession, counsel, and absolution, has of course to be private, but most of it cries out to be done surrounded by the visible fellowship of the Church. To see a person who is ill receiving Communion and the laying on of hands with twelve members of the Mothers' Union present is to come to a fresh realization of what the Church as the Body of Christ really means. Most of the regular weekly sick communicants have celebrations once a month in their own homes, and other members of the Church come to join in the services to bring them the fellowship of the Church. The same should happen where possible at the laying on of hands and the anointing.

The congregation is to be encouraged to realize that those who are not able to come to church for one reason or another are very much their brothers and sisters in Christ. One of our sick Communion folk has never been able to come inside St. Wilfrid's, although it has been consecrated seventeen years, but she very much feels an integral part of the Church. This has been because she has regularly received Communion reserved at the Parish Communion on Sunday morning, and has been the 'hostess' to several house celebrations with wonderful gatherings of Church people round her bed-side. She was also one of the first to have a people's service in the house immediately after Sunday Evensong. In these ways the Church is built up, is built up as a healing fellowship.

'Fetch a doctor' is quite commonplace, but in the Church of England sending for a priest is sometimes the last resort when all else has failed. Here there is certainly room for a radical change of attitude and much scope for team-work between doctor, priest, relations, Christian friends, and the patient. A bottle of medicine or an injection of penicillin can work miracles. But so can a 'bottle' of prayer or an 'injection' of Communion. The prayers of the Church and the laying on of hands with prayer can be regarded as part of the normal healing ministry. Many doctors would like to use bottles of medicine much less, but they are often the victims of their patients who don't think them any good unless they give them medicine, a continual variety of medicines. There is a need for an increasing team spirit amongst all those who are involved in healing.

We need to surround our beds of sickness with faith. We need to surround our death beds with faith. I believe we need bands of people who are prepared to meet in the church building or in homes to pray for those who are sick. We need people who are prepared to go round to visit the sick. We need people who are prepared to be trained to visit the sick and expound the Bible and co-operate in the laying on of hands. We need, above all, to help patients' relations and friends to see their vocation as healers, to see their vocation to surround the sick bed by faith and prayer and not by hopeless or stoical sorrow.

The Church is a healing fellowship and the vocation of the Christian congregation is to build up the right attitude of faith, hope, and charity, so that Christ can heal to-day. Lord Eustace Percy's words come alive:

> The more the congregation becomes a healing one, the more it realizes its vocation to be a healing fellowship, to be the Body of Christ. And the more it will see what healing power Christians have to give to a half-destroyed world.

The more the Church becomes the Body of Christ, the more the Church will see the need for 'the revival of the Christian congregation.' The aim of the Christian congregation reaches out to touch all men with its healing life of fellowship. The Christian congregation is to rouse the response of the individual that he may understand,

and, through understanding, may co-operate in the spirit of expectancy in faith.

We cannot think of sickness and disease without considering death. For mortal sinful man it is the final point in the sojourn here on earth which is our preparation for eternal life. It is one of the points at which team-work sometimes breaks down. Doctors and relations often agree that if a person is dying he should not be told. If people don't believe in an after life there certainly is something to be said for this attitude. If people believe in this life only, it is obvious that the main aim is to stay alive in this world as long as possible. But if we believe in God and a life after death which goes on beyond this life, is it not right that people should be prepared for death as far as possible? Should they not have an opportunity to grow as much as possible in the last six months, three months, three days, three hours, before their death? Why should they not be told? Most of the desire to keep the truth out is dishonesty and reflects a lack of faith; none knows when death is going to come, and there is always amazing evidence of how those given up by doctors have recovered through their own faith or the faith of friends and relations.

We are increasingly seeing our responsibility towards the 'four wheelers.' We have considered those who are brought in the pram to be baptized, we have considered those who are brought in a taxi to be married, but we have not yet considered those who are brought in a hearse to be buried. What is happening in the building up of the Church as the Body of Christ will help towards a different attitude towards death. The Burial Service must be given a meaning—it certainly hasn't one now in the minds of thousands who have the Prayer Book Service when they die. The long-term policy is that all baptized people should have a Communion service at their burial. But of course most people do not expect it, and even to many regular communicants the idea seems strange, even more strange than having a Communion service at their marriage. The matter has to be dealt with much further back than the death bed. The death bed without Communion reminds us of Baptism without Confirmation and Communion. The more that people see that membership is fulfilled in communicant membership, the more people will see the Communion service as the centre of their lives. It is as the people see the Communion service as the centre of their lives week by week that they will not be without it, on special occasions as well as on ordinary occasions. People are instructed so as to be able to receive Communion; people are confirmed so as to be able to receive Communion; people receive Communion at their wedding, week by week in their homes, on their sick beds, on their death beds: and their funeral happens in the setting of Communion. And all this is because they are baptized, they are inheritors of the kingdom of heaven: the Communion at the burial and the continued intercession of the Church make the last stage of our Baptism follow-up by the Church on earth.

It is as the congregation becomes aware of itself as a eucharistic fellowship that Communion will be seen as the 'done' thing: the 'done thing' at all the great events of life, as it is the 'done thing' on the first day of every week; it will be seen as the way in which men are to keep the Sabbath holy, and to keep the whole of life holy, to put God in the centre of life, and in the centre of the world.

## CHAPTER X

# *CHURCH UNITY*

ALL Christian bodies are lacking in wholeness; all are sick—as Canon Oliver Tomkins reminds us in his book, *The Wholeness of the Church*. Therefore we all need each other. The Ecumenical Movement is the movement of the Holy Spirit in which we are discovering each other as fellow Christians, and discovering as fellow Christians how much we need each other, and discovering how much we can learn from each other, how much we can grow together, while apart.

We cannot build up the Church inside or outside the church building and ignore the fact that there are other Christians from whom we are separated, who gather together for worship, who organize their life and witness, quite apart from us and from each other. I believe we cannot go on doing this without ignoring Christ. Canon Oliver Tomkins at the Lund Conference challenged all of us when he said that we must do together everything except those things which we must according to conscience do separately. This approach to the scandal of our unhappy divisions is unknown in the ordinary parish; the Ecumenical Movement, which Archbishop Temple described as 'the great new fact of our era,' must develop grass roots; I believe that at the house level we are next door to the Ecumenical conversation.

May I again quote Dr. J. A. T. Robinson on his experience here at Halton

of a form of the Church different from that which most people in this country have ever actually known. And it is a form which compels those who find themselves within it to face questions which other levels of Christian living still allow them to evade. When there is no church to *go* to, one can only *be* the Church. At this level there is a new constraint both towards mission and towards involvement in Christ. One cannot ignore either the house next door (there is no 'next door' to the parish church) or the Christian next to one (the parlour is very different from the pew).

In this form of the Church, too, the challenge of disunity comes with fresh force. Where most of the *superficial* differences disappear and men of the same household still find themselves divided, the 'why' and the 'how long' press with more insistent reality. At the same time there is being built up in the house-church something much less vulnerable to disintegration from *without*. In the event of persecution the Church does not have to go underground: it is underground, even if the super-structure has to go.

The house-church faces us with the challenge of our dislikes and distrusts within our own Church. If the Church is to be a fellowship of reconciliation it must really get to grips with the personal failures of charity among its own members by which the world judges us so severely. The house celebration has helped here: the force of the invitation to confession often comes home more seriously round a kitchen table than in the bigger Parish Communion congregation. Neighbours who have fallen out and who have come quite comfortably to the church building have seen that they cannot attend a house celebration in their neighbourhood without first healing the breach.

In the house-church we realize a bit more of what it means to be a parochial church, the church of a specific area: this is the basis of our mission as Anglicans. But how much mistrust, or at least ignorance, there is between the churches of neighbouring parishes, especially in towns! There is a tremendous need for a unity movement within the Church of England. The Minneapolis Con-gress did this, but it still has to be made local. The Provost of Bradford has been holding week-end conferences at Swanwick for the northern dioceses under the title of 'It begins in the parish.' A condition of attendance has been that no clergyman can come without some of his laity, and no lay people may come without their clergyman. Realizing that this was still not yet local enough, our diocese has organized some week-end conferences at our diocesan house for teams to meet from neighbouring parishes. Three impressions stand out specially from the conference that Halton went to: (1) that we were astonishingly ignorant about each other as parishes; (2) that most of the things that we get worked up about in Halton are the concerns of the other parishes too; (3) that we had all grown most usefully into being the Church by means of some weakness or failure. So we have been learning to be honest and trusting with each other as Anglicans and we have been trying to build up real trust between parish and parish, between priest and people.

In the house-church we are all near enough to our fellow Christians of other denominations to meet in a new and vital way. Whether the Roman Catholics co-operate or not, I believe we must take risks and go on facing up to the scandal of our unhappy divisions. The high priestly prayer of our Lord, 'That they all may be one that the world might believe,' must be ever before us in the house-church. The disunity of the Church, I believe, is one of the biggest factors that prevents the lapsed baptized and the outsider generally from seeing the charity of God. It is not only intellectual enthusiasts like Victor Gollancz that are prepared to listen to Christ, but are not prepared to listen to Him in the Church. 'See how these Christians love one another' is still the acid test of our Christianity and until we are fully charitable one towards the other we must be working and slaving towards that end. Studdert Kennedy once said that we must have a 'pain in the mind.' We need to be concerned about the mangled Body of Christ. Concerned that people are turned away from Christ, not only in our parish, but in Africa, India, West Indies, in every part of the world, because of our divisions.

'We must be loyal to the truth in our own fragmentation and we must be willing to learn the truth from other fragmentations' (Oliver Tomkins). In divided Christendom we need to learn from each other. In divided Christendom we are learning that if there is something that we consider to be inadequate or lacking in truth in another confession we share the blame; because the Church is divided, each confession is incomplete in its worship and in its theology and in its witness to the uniting power of Christ. In divided Christendom we must learn to be humble and penitent. As we work in a parish the work of Christ and His Church is increasingly sending our folk out to the frontier. In the Church at the house level I find myself increasingly saying—if only the witness of the Methodists was being made at this point, if only the witness of the Roman Catholics was being made at that point, if only the witness of the Quakers, of the Salvation Army, of the Orthodox, if only the witness of the Baptists, if only the witness of the Congregationalists; I find myself going further still and saying, if only the witness of the Jews, particularly the way in which the Jews have maintained religion in the home—they have always made the home the centre of their religion, with the father as the priest in his own home. The door is still open for Elijah on Friday night, the candles are lit and the youngest member able to ask still says, 'What mean ye by this service?'

Yes, what a lot we have to learn from each other. And where are we to learn it if not in our own street? Here we are next door to the Ecumenical challenge, for here we may have a Roman Catholic next door on one side and a Methodist on the other, and a Jew next door to the Roman Catholic and a Communist next to the Jew. At the street level we can ask the question, 'Are we the Body of Christ or just a group of people who go to the church building?' If we are just a group of people who go to a church building, then we can go on building up our own particular denomination and ignore the others. We can go on attending services, singing hymns, and attending the men's meeting and the women's bright hour and the youth fellowship, we can go on teaching the children Bible stories; but if we believe we go to the church building to become the Body of Christ, then we realize we cannot be the Body of Christ divided from other groups of Christians in the area. They are called to worship the same Christ. We cannot ignore these other Christians without ignoring Christ. There is a *must* about our worship, but our worship is a fragmentation of the worship of the Body of Christ. We must meet as Christians to rehearse what great things God has done. We cannot meet and ignore other Christians who are meeting. Bishop Gore reminded us that he who is not in heart and mind a missionary is no Christian. Very often it seems to be left to the fundamentalist groups to display real missionary enthusiasm to-day: I believe that we have much to learn from them too, and I want to give my testimony to the concern for souls and the Christian fellowship that I experienced in serving on the Leeds Billy Graham Committee. The mission of the Church is one, whether at home or overseas. We cannot fully witness to Christ in divided Christendom. There is a divine imperative about doing something to remove the obstacles which prevent the Church being the Church, being the Body of Christ.

Evanston reminds us that

the call to evangelism, therefore, must be addressed first of all to the Churches themselves—awakening them to a renewal of their own inner life. Judgement does begin at the household of God. 'It is urgent,' the report asserts, 'that the Church come to life in small neighbourhoods, e.g. in "street or house churches" where neighbours, church and non-church, gather to think and pray.' In other words, experiencing the new life with God offered in the gospel is a requisite for receiving witnessing power. The Church must offer this in recognizable forms. It cannot be had in isolation. We need fellowship—the fellowship of the Holy Spirit—in 'upper rooms' where two or three are gathered together in His Name, so that He can be in the midst of us.[1]

What is needed is a new attitude towards mission and unity and community. Oliver Tomkins, in his book, *The Wholeness of the Church*, reminds us how much unity, community, and evangelism are bound up together.

We cannot build up the Church as a community without relating that community to those who are outside the worshipping community, and that is evangelism. We cannot make an impact on the whole community as long as there are several worshipping congregations trying to do the same thing. The more we realize this the more we are driven to work for unity; and the more we do this the more we see that the challenge of the Church throughout the world and the challenge of the Church in the local situation are one and the same.

There is an attitude which excludes Rome and there is an attitude which excludes Protestants, when we consider the unity of the Church. Both states of mind are equally non-Ecumenical. Here is an illustration, which shows a closed mind. An address at a fraternal on unity was divided into two parts; the first part was the condemnation of the South India scheme, very well worked out and convincing. The second part advocated keeping the door open to Rome and three main points were made. (1) The Holy Spirit is at work in the Roman Church today, and there are signs of a change of outlook in many places, chiefly in France. (2) We must exercise real charity towards the Roman Church. (3) We don't really understand the Romans until we see them at worship. After the talk I said that I couldn't agree more with the latter half of the address; it was backed up by what I had seen and experienced in Colombes, in Montreuil, in L'Hayla Roses, and what I have read of the Mission to Paris and Mission to France, and the work of the Little Brothers and

[1] *Evanston Speaks*, p. 29.

Little Sisters of Jesus of Charles de Foucauld.[1] This made one thank God for the Holy Spirit and the way He is working wonders in the Roman Church. It is true that when one meets people like the Abbé Michonneau or the Abbé Couturier one realizes what a great sympathy and understanding there is in the Roman Church and how we must exercise real charity with the local Romans. We must exercise charity with local Romans and learn to speak the truth in love. How true it is that it is when we enter into each other's worship that we see the Ecumenical Movement, and there is certainly a richness in Roman worship which has its contribution to make in the Ecumenical Movement. But I asked the speaker the question—if this is to be true of our attitude towards Rome, why not to the Protestants? Are we to deny that the Holy Spirit is working in the Protestant Church? Are we to deny that He has still work to do through them? If we learn to understand Romans by entering into their worship, are we not to understand Protestants by entering into their worship? I did not think the fullness of worship was represented at the Dutch Reformed Lord's Supper at Amsterdam in 1939, when they sat down round a table one hundred at a time and the bread was passed round and the cup shared while we sang 'O Sacred Head Sore Wounded.' But as we have discovered here in Halton something of the need to be the Church in the parish church and to be the Church in the house-church, we have also come to appreciate what the Protestants have to say about the worship at the Eucharist. The meaning of 'We do not presume to come to this Thy table' has been enriched by that experience.

As we have come to realize the meaning of the Eucharist we have seen more and more the point of gathering round the family table for this meal. The liturgical details are not the important things, the important thing is that we

[1] A Little Brother came to one of our home meetings and said, after a long discussion, 'It was our fault at the Reformation.' There are only two answers to this: either, 'Yes, of course it was,' or 'It was our fault too.'

should give glory and worship and honour and praise to God. The important thing is that we should be loyal to our own fragmentation of worship and be prepared to learn from other fragmentations.

Here at Halton during a Week of Unity we tried to put into practice what Archbishop Temple said, that we do not understand each other unless we have attended each other's characteristic form of worship. On January 18, 1953, our Methodist people attended our Parish Communion, and we attended their morning worship, which included a public Baptism! On the second Sunday the Congregational people did the same. On neither occasion was there any question of communicating, but we certainly felt the scandal that we didn't communicate, and we certainly did grow in our understanding of each other. This was an attempt to enter into each other's characteristic form of worship. This was our attempt to understand something of what we do when we worship. During the week we had three inter-Church meetings, on the parish meeting, the class meeting, and the church meeting. This was our attempt to understand how we express our congregational life outside the worship in church. Also during the week we held fourteen interdenominational home meetings. This was our attempt to get alongside each other in the Name of the Lord. If we had not developed the house-church and been meeting regularly in homes these interdenominational meetings would never have taken place. We saw during this week the need for holding a regular church-society-parish meeting to discover what the Holy Spirit is saying to the divided Church in Halton. During this week we were attempting to be concerned in prayer and meeting and action about the disunity of the Church, that the world may believe. We had our meeting with the local Member of Parliament on the final Sunday night speaking on 'The Christian in International Affairs,' and we were left with no shadow of doubt about the responsibility of the Christian to be concerned with the world that God made. The most important thing during the week was not what was said, but what was done—the fact that we have met each other in our church buildings, in our halls, and in our homes as members of worshipping fellowships and as fellow Christians. We were encouraged during the week by the prayers of the local Roman Catholics. Never at any time in our thinking and praying for unity is it right for us to leave the Roman Catholics out. We remember with gratitude the words of the late Abbé Couturier:

> Faced with the sad realities in the world to-day the Christian, be he Catholic or Protestant, Orthodox or Anglican, must of necessity act, and there is only one action that is adequate in the present situation and that is the action of prayer.

Here is the programme for the Week of Unity in Halton, 1954, following up attending each other's morning worship in 1953 by attending each other's Communion service.

THEME OF THE WEEK: 'In order to unite with one another we must love one another, in order to love one another we must know one another, in order to know one another we must meet one another' (Cardinal Mercier). Let us meet this week in the Name of the Lord because we must meet. We betray our Lord if we don't meet. Let us pray with our Lord 'That all may be one that the world may believe.' Let us see what Canon Oliver Tomkins means when he says we must do together everything except that which is against conscience. We have hardly begun to do this in this area yet.

Sunday, January 17th.

6.00 p.m. Interchange of pulpits—the Rev. F. Brock and the Vicar.

7.30 p.m. United Covenant Service at the Methodist Church.

Monday, January 18th.

7.45 p.m. United Men's Rally at Congregational Church. Speaker: The Rev. R. Kissack, Brunswick Methodist Church.

Tuesday, January 19th.
8.00 p.m. Interdenominational Home Meetings.

Wednesday, January 20th.
8.00 p.m. Inter-Church Meeting at St. Wilfrid's Hall. Speaker: The Rev. H. Morton (Methodist), S.C.M. Secretary, Leeds University.

Thursday, January 21st.
2.45 p.m. Women's Rally at Methodist Hall. Speaker: The Rev. D. Rogers (Congregationalist).
8.00 p.m. Interdenominational Home Meetings.

Friday, January 22nd.
2.30 p.m. Women's Home Meetings.
8.00 p.m. Interdenominational Home Meetings and Youth Home Meetings. (Interdenominational choir practice with Fr. Lev Gillet (Eastern Orthodox) at 7 p.m. at St. Wilfrid's Church, before the Home Meetings.)

Saturday, January 23rd.
7.00 a.m. Orthodox Liturgy—celebrated by Fr. Lev Gillet of the Fellowship of St. Alban and St. Sergius. Please make a super-human effort to be present!!

CONFERENCE—
2.30 p.m. Opening Prayers at St. Wilfrid's.
2.45 p.m. Address by Canon Oliver Tomkins, Principal of Lincoln Theological College, formerly Assoc.-Gen. Secretary of the World Council of Churches. *Subject:* 'The Wholeness of the Church.'
3.30 p.m. Groups.
4.00 p.m. Open Forum to answer questions.
4.45 p.m. Home for tea.
6.30 p.m. Free Church Celebration of the Holy Communion at the Congregational Church. (Members of the Church of England will attend as observers but will not communicate.)
7.30 p.m. Conference continued. Speaker: Fr. Lev Gillet—'Orthodox Worship.'

Sunday, January 24th.
9.00 a.m. Communion at St. Wilfrid's Church. Preacher: Canon Oliver Tomkins. (All Free Church people invited to attend as observers.)

6.00 p.m. Interchange of pulpits—the Rev. R. Parmley and the Vicar.

7.45 p.m. Rally at St. Wilfrid's. Speaker: Fr. Lev Gillet—'The Orthodox Church in the World Church.'

Monday, January 25th.

7.30 p.m. Mass Rally at the Church Institute. Chairman: The Bishop of Ripon. Speaker: The Rev. Leonard Schiff. *Subject:* 'The Church of South India.'

Tuesday, January 26th.

7.00 a.m. Liturgy of the Church of South India—celebrated by the Rev. Leonard Schiff in St. Wilfrid's.

At Halton during this week we learned and relearned the truth that:

We owe our home meetings in part to the Methodists;
We owe our parish meeting in part to the Congregationalists;
We owe our offertory procession in part to the Eastern Orthodox;
We owe our concern about Baptism in part to the Baptists;
We owe our concern about Communion in part to the Roman Catholics;
We owe our concern about prayer in part to the Quakers.

During the week we learned what a lot we had still to learn about ourselves and each other, and we learned under the Holy Spirit that it all takes time and it all takes faith and penitence and humility. At the end of the week there seemed so much for which to thank God and take courage after ten years praying and working for local Ecumenism. Here at Halton we are discovering Amsterdam, Lund, Travancore, and Evanston writ small.

The last paragraph was an extract from a note on the back of our Church Council agenda for February, 1954. As a result of the Week of Unity we decided that we must keep on learning from each other at the house level. Meeting each other in homes we found that before we are Methodists and Congregationalists and Anglicans we are primarily people in touch with the saving power of God in Christ, Who is gathering all men unto Himself in His Church, the community of the Holy Spirit: we saw that the most important thing about us is that we are one. But this did not make us cheerful and careless about our divisions: on the contrary, we saw all the more clearly how serious they are, how intolerable that man's pride and unconcern should hinder Christ from making His Church free to be a fully reconciling and redeeming agency. We saw that the Ecumenical Movement will be untrue to its calling unless it continues and grows as a movement of repentance; so it seemed to many of us that until as Churches we are more prepared for a corporate dying into one Church we shall be wrong to anticipate our unity in promoting intercommunion. But as we go on meeting in each other's homes, we feel driven to work more seriously for the time when we shall also be able to break bread together; there we *may* discover that this is the point at which our Lord is preparing us to break bread together.

We must steadily go on meeting and doing things together: so we formed the Halton Council of Churches, not to assemble the keen people and so excuse the rest of our congregation, but to plan and work on behalf of us all. We held the first meeting of the Halton Council of Churches at the vicarage in March, 1954. The ministers and clergy of Halton Methodist, Congregationalist, and St. Wilfrid's Churches were present, with four lay representatives from each and representatives from the Area Council of Churches and Toc H; Miss Ilse Friedeberg from the Ecumenical Institute, Bossey, and Mr. Michael Butterfield, one of the Evanston delegates, were there as visitors.

At this meeting we decided to hold regular interdenominational home meetings. These were held in April, during the visit of the Rev. John Perret; in May, during a Healing Week-end, conducted by the Rev. Jim Wilson, Chaplain of the Guild of Health; in June, when we were sharing in a week of preparation for the Second Assembly of the World Council of Churches by considering in the homes the same themes that the delegates would be discussing at Evanston (the Rev. Harry Morton, S.C.M. Secretary at Leeds University, was with us this week): in July, during the visit of Mr. Michael Butterfield; in September, to meet our M.P., Mr. Denis Healey; in October, during the visit of the Rev. Dewi Morgan of the Society for the Propagation of the Gospel; in December, with the Town Clerk of Harrogate; in January, during the Week of Unity, conducted by the Rev. Kenneth Slack, Secretary of the British Council of Churches; in February, with Major Brooksbank, one of our city councillors.

We also decided to send representatives to the Whitsun Conference of the British Council of Churches at Swanwick, and to meet the local branch of the United Nations Association to discuss the question of race with Brother Roger of the Community of the Resurrection.

We agreed to show our united witness in a procession on Good Friday from the Congregational Church past the Methodist Church, through the housing estates to St. Wilfrid's for a united service.

A combined social was arranged for a Saturday at the Congregational Schoolroom.

The Evanston Congress presupposed that there was a local Ecumenical fellowship to work its discussions out at the local level; this is what we were trying to do in Halton.

I want to underline where we have got to by including some recommendations which were accepted on the final Sunday of our Week of Unity in 1955.

(i) We believe that we have been called by God into a vital relationship with each other in the Ecumenical Movement.

(ii) We believe that we have already been led to grow together in Halton—thanks be to God. And we believe we are called to go forward with deeper penitence and deeper faith—Lord, hear our prayer.

(iii) We believe that at the present time we must 'let the Week of Unity interfere with our denominational activity' so that we can give priority to prayer and meeting together during that week—a foretaste of things to come.

(iv) We believe that, at the present time, we should go on meeting regularly in each other's homes, but on a different day of the week each month, so that people who are, rightly, supporting their own church meetings and other activities may attend them.

(v) We believe that we ought to be exploring further the possibilities of entering into each other's activities; for example, Bible study, prayer meetings, church meetings, joint visiting, and so on, as well as our men's, women's, and youth work.

(vi) We believe that we ought to be exploring further joint service to the community—everything from old people's services to inter-Church aid and refugee work.

We would agree with Canon Tomkins that most of our congregation's activity is organized as if the others did not exist. And that is as far as we have got in ten years. There is no short cut, I believe, to this local co-operation. There is no substitute for prayer and slog and tremendous patience. And in practice we shall find that we must do most of our growing together while apart.

Does it all sound very dangerous? Some would say that only Church leaders can be allowed to engage in the Ecumenical Movement, that the ordinary layman cannot be trusted. What a counsel of despair! Here we are, encouraging and trying to equip our laymen to do the fantastically difficult job of presenting the Christian Gospel to those who are outside the Church, and we boggle at the idea of letting them meet their fellow-Christians! We must train ourselves for this meeting, of course, for the work can be served only by those who are responsible members of their own Church and value beyond measure the particular riches which the Holy Spirit has entrusted to it. This is no task for the rootless and vague, any more than is the outward mission of the Church. In Halton this drove us in Lent, 1955, to study the Minneapolis Report in six parish meetings under the title of 'Why be an Anglican?'—the one answer that won't do is 'Why not?'!

If we believe in the Holy Ghost, in the Holy Catholic Church, then we must believe that the Ecumenical Movement is the great new fact of our era, then it must become the great new fact in our local areas. Evanston speaks clearly, Christ speaks through Evanston to us, and He says love and go on and on loving one another, remembering, as Dostoyevsky tells us, that love in action is a terrifying and a crucifying experience.

We come to see that, in faith and penitence, we must all humble ourselves before God and each other. We must implore other Christians and other denominations to come and help us. We need you. Without you, the particular truth that God has given us turns to a lie and becomes a barrier. For in truth we *are* one, not because 'we're all heading for the same place,' not because 'we all believe the same thing really,' not because it would save money or help our evangelism if we were one. No: we are one simply and solely because God has made us one and Jesus is gathering all men unto Himself. He, not we, made the Church. Whether we like it or not He is attracting men to Himself, and giving them His fellowship and there is only one of Him. Nothing that man can do can smash His unity. 'Man can conceal it or reveal it, but he can neither create it nor destroy it.'[1]

So this Church unity movement is firstly God trying to get man to reveal to the world a unity which He has made and intended long ago; as we go on we realize this more and more seriously. Our work together is more than just book learning and exchange of ideas, or a chance to score points: we are to grow into a mood of responsible penitence instead of cheerful uneasiness, a mood of determination to be tiresome and tireless and restless and

[1] Oliver Tomkins in an address at Swanwick, 1954.

dissatisfied until the Church has enough holiness and urgency of mission for Christ to entrust to it the visible unity that He longs to give it. In all this we believe that it is at the house level that we are providing the sort of environment in which the precious gift of unity can be given to the Church.

## CHAPTER XI

# *AM I MY BROTHER'S KEEPER?*

THE world situation is the local situation writ large and the local situation is the world situation writ small. It is so easy to get worked up emotionally about a film on leprosy or yaws, or about atomic warfare, and at the same time to do very little about it. Often there seems so little we can do about it, even if we want to. But the acid test of our concern for our brother is our concern for him in our own locality.

In the leaflet published for the United Nations Association Exhibition, *The Way Ahead*, there is a drawing of mountain peaks entitled 'War' and 'Want'; the subtitle is 'Unconquered Still.' War is one of the unconquered peaks. The leaflet reminds us that all the world is frightened, and most of the world is sick, half the world is hungry, half the world is illiterate; and it points out that the way ahead to peace is through the United Nations, through the Food and Agriculture Organization and U.N.I.C.E.F., through the U.N.'s Educational Scientific, and Cultural Organization. The great missionary societies of the Church have, of course, been working to that end for a very long time, and would do much more if they had more support. They are an inescapable obligation of every Christian, commanded by our Lord Himself.

We must start backing all this up by making it more local.

Many people are frightened in our own area, many people are ill, many are hungry, many are ignorant, many people in our area are not contributing to the peaceful settlement of disputes—in their own family, in their own street, in their own parish. We are to build up peace in our own area, we are to build up health in our own area, we are to build up knowledge in our own area. So we are to build up the local Church in our own area, and we are to proclaim that war, disease, hunger, and ignorance are the work of the devil. We can't get complete peace and health and food and knowledge apart from the kingdom of God. The Church Assembly Report, *Towards a Common Life*, has one of its main chapters on the local community.

The Church is a community with a common life whose source is God. . . . They share it because they are made members in Baptism, and their membership means that they have one heart and soul. In the early Church the evidence of this was marked and led to practical demonstrations that they had all things in common. . . . It may be true that the voluntary Communism of the early Church was a 'piece of economic folly' as Dr. Lionel Thornton says it was.[1]

But unfortunately the present-day Church gives little evidence of holding the belief that prompted the experiment to be made.

It is the attitude of mind which needs changing so that we expect the Church to be different and help the Church to be different. 'It seemed good to the Holy Spirit and to us' is not the sort of thing that the Church finds easy to say to-day. Nor is there always a meeting of the Church to say it in any case. Is the worshipping community indeed a fellowship, and does it realize its vocation to be a fellowship? It is as we realize more what our worship really means that we shall deep down come to grips with ourselves as 'our brother's keeper.'

Since the issues of the local community's life are so much affected by the national policy and national purposes, it will be inevitable that both local and national issues will prove to be ever-recurring subjects of discussion.

In any parish group or parish meeting which is really trying to be the expression of the Church's community life,

[1] *Towards a Common Life*, p. 40: this report has received far less attention than it deserves.

it will be found impossible to isolate the problems of parochial and pastoral life from the problem of wider societies; such meetings will provide opportunities for clarifying the thoughts of members about the issues which affect the life of the Church and nation.

A group of Christian people who have together worried out the implications of some of the features of national or local life, and who have arrived at a common mind, will be a greater power than a number of people who hold similar opinions but who have had no opportunity for testing them or bringing the mind of the Church to bear on them.

Attempts to do the kind of thing suggested here must not be confused with the attempts to make the Church 'more efficient' by having a multiplicity of organizations. There may be such organizations but the Parish Communion and the parish meeting will gather up their life.

The Parish Communion and the parish meeting are means by which the Church might be helped to fulfil its mission of teaching people how to live and work together. It is paradoxical to talk of creating spontaneous community and of course we cannot create it, but God can create it where we use the means He has given to us. Even then, the worship and the work must be addressed to God and not be fashioned to achieve some purpose on which we have set our hearts.

But the absence of a sense of fellowship in the Church at all approaching the New Testament *koinonia* should not be attributed merely to changed social conditions. It is due to the inferior quality of Christians and to the fact that in our worship and Church social life we are seeking less to do the will of God than to maintain the Church as an efficient organization.

Although the Church intends her worship to be addressed to God, it is too often measured by the pleasure it gives to those who take part in its services, and organizations—valuable though many of them are in stressing some aspect of the Church's teaching—may tend to break up the fellowship of the family of the parish church.

If the work and worship of the Church are done for God, certain results will follow. One of them will be that the Church will show the meaning of what it is to have all things in common and to be of one heart and soul.[1]

[1] Op. cit., p. 44.

It is perfectly true that it is not sufficient for Christians to be interested in chasubles and not in drains—to be interested in the sanctuary and not to be interested in politics—to be interested in reading the Bible but not interested in world poverty—to be interested in pews in church but not to be interested in good housing: we must discover the connection between all things in the Lord.

Here are two illustrations amongst many others. In our parish there are boys who never get away for a holiday, and sometimes they include boys who are on probation. Five years ago the Rector of Spennithorne, the Rev. J. Jory, and myself conceived the idea of taking three or four dozen of these boys, aged 11–15, away to the country for a fortnight. Spennithorne, a village in Wensleydale, now means a new way of looking at life for dozens of lads. In the last two years an extra week has been added for those boys who have now started work, and the Spennithorne boys are in the heart of our youth club at St. Wilfrid's. This particular link with Spennithorne and the general fellowship between the parishes provide one of our most worthwhile experiences of the Church. During 1955 in addition to the camp a bus-load of our folk went up to Spennithorne to join in their Rogation procession round the parish, and a bus-load of Spennithorne folk came down to have a folk-dancing evening with us in Halton.

Again, our branch of the Anglican Young People's Association realized in 1954 that it was not sufficient for it to come up to the church building every Friday night to meet: it had to represent the Church getting out into the world around to work wherever there was need. The old people in our parish live mostly in five definite areas, so the A.Y.P.A. started to visit these areas systematically to find out who needed what: some jobs the members did themselves—particularly redecorating old people's flats; other needs were passed on to the clergy, for visiting, sick Communion, and so on, or to other members of the congregation, for radio repairs or shopping. The parish has benefited by this, of course, but so has the Church—it has found itself in another way as the Church in action, the Church with as definite a job as any political party: Christian service is the one language of the Church that the outsider can understand. This was no sudden discovery, for Christians have been doing work for people in various ways all along, and the Church has been playing its part in working for the various needs of the community. But this work by the A.Y.P.A. led to the main report at the annual meeting in 1955 being on the subject of social service, and since then this has become a definite part of parish policy—one in which there is also a great opportunity for co-operating with other Christians. In the Ecumenical work camps the World Council of Churches has given a relatively small number of people a wonderful experience of being drawn together by the needs of the world: this also has to be made local, and it may turn out to be a bit more difficult to work with our neighbours round the corner than with a Lutheran from Eastern Germany or a Methodist from the Philippines.

Organizations attached to the church building have their place, but the danger is that people will be involved in 'church work' and not see that they are to go out into the world to serve God faithfully, still in the fellowship of the Church. I remember so well in a Durham pit village during the time of unemployment between the wars a young shop assistant saying to me, 'You've no idea how difficult it is to make my counter my altar.' There is a danger in seeing only a part of life as part of God's world. It was a very salutary reply which the baker gave; when asked what church work he did, he replied, 'I bake.'

When I look at the Baptism register and see the occupations of the fathers who have had their babies baptized, I see here the key to evangelism. *The* task of evangelism is to show these fathers that their own Baptism and the Baptism of their children is related to their daily work and intimately bound up with every problem, national and international. Christ is the Lord of history, or He isn't Lord at all. One of the movements which is helping the Church to see the true implications of this is the Sheffield Industrial Mission, under the Bishop of Sheffield and Canon Ted Wickham: in Halton we have been encouraged a lot by their steady and penetrating work of discovery, and we have been trying to translate their findings and experience into the every-day policy of a parish. We go to the church building to learn to worship and to learn obedience, then we go out to worship and to obey.

This obedience includes political obedience. Before the 1950 General Election we decided to have a meeting and we invited both the candidates to answer our questions, which were based on the claim of Christ over the whole life of man. At the meeting the first thing we had to do was to introduce the candidates to each other. It was good that a Church gathering was the means whereby they were brought together on the same platform. We began with prayer and reading from Scripture and before the introduction of the candidates something was said about the heresy of separating Christianity from politics or anything else. The two candidates spoke for twenty minutes each and then the questions were put to them. These and other questions put from the floor were answered alternately by the candidates in the presence of about two hundred people. Before the end of the meeting representatives of both parties (Conservative and Labour) expressed very real appreciation to the parish church for providing such a platform on which they could meet, and the campaign which began the very next day was a very clean one. Many attributed this to the send-off from the parish church. One of the local political leaders at the end of the meeting reminded us all that this was what the Church ought to be doing, this was not the Church saying just 'come to church,' but being the

Church and claiming the whole of the life of man for God. He also went on to say that the parish meeting was a regular feature of the parish, and that this was the place in the parish where men and women could come and meet each other, whatever their political colour. He also made a plea for Christians to come in and take a responsible part in political leadership.

Certainly this was an opportunity for the candidates to meet the Church. Meanwhile there have been similar opportunities for our M.P. to meet the Church. From January 18 to 25, 1953, we held a series of inter-denominational parish meetings and home meetings. On the final night our M.P. spoke on 'A Christian in International Affairs.' He helped us to see that we are all members of both the realm of the Spirit and the realm of Caesar, and that our membership of one must vitally affect our membership of the other: we must let the love-motive of Christianity control and turn to good use the power-motive of politics and of many other human associations: we must never try to keep the two motives immaculately apart. His talk was itself a specimen of how Christian wisdom provides the equipment for really understanding what makes men and countries act as they do; Christian honesty makes us see things as they are in fact, instead of the encouraging fiction that 'we' are all St. George and 'they' are all the dragon. The Christian should be able to see things honestly and realistically: politics, both national and international, are often dishonest and unrealistic; but this is all the more reason why the Christian should be really involved in Caesar's world and not pretend that he has nothing to do with it.

The important thing about this was that we provided an environment in which a conversation took place between an M.P. and a body of Christian people in this area.

For the 1955 election we had another meeting for the candidates, this time under the auspices of the Halton

Council of Churches. Each year our M.P. and our city councillors come round and meet the Church in the house. Thus can the Church and the politician each learn from the other.

How are we to keep on learning at the local level? Bishop Frank Weston said we must relate the two communities, the congregation and the parish, otherwise we make nonsense of the Gospel. I believe we can do this best by getting alongside each other in our own street. We are right in the midst of social responsibility. We may be next door to an agnostic, or a Communist, and so we are right in the midst of the warfare of ideologies. If we are alive to our responsibility for the person next door then we are more likely to see that next door to the next door but one can lead us out to our responsibilities in Kenya and Johannesburg and Cyprus.

Recently we have been discussing the booklet, *Time to Wake Up*, published by the Association for World Peace. We saw the question, 'One world or two?' in its relationship to our own neighbourhood. We saw that one of the answers to the bench marked 'European only' in South Africa is to build up a deeper responsibility for our neighbours in our own street. We saw that we could help by our prayers and by our reading of the Bible, by giving our money, by our conversation at work, by our witness in trade unions, club, guild, group, and so on, by being involved in the United Nations Organization through the nearest branch of the United Nations Association. We are often put to shame by the concern and care for the needs of the world that is shown by people who never come to church: we of the Church must get alongside them, listen to them, catch some of their concern and link it up with our Christian way of seeing things.

In Halton this has had a direct affect on the local U.N.A. itself; it now arranges a series of home meetings every other month to study some department of U.N.O. work such as the Food and Agriculture Organization or some particular problem of international affairs such as Formosa or Cyprus. Here there has been a real chance for Christians and non-Christians to learn from each other as they are drawn together by their common concern for the world. In the home, people meet each other primarily as people rather than as representatives of this or that 'ism,' in an encounter of experience and opinion in a growing fellowship of learning. It is obvious that political parties largely depend for their support and independence on traditional distrusts and suspicions of each other, and this spirit often maintains denominational separations too. Ultimately this can never bring true strength, healing, and peace to the world or to the Church: it is in continual personal meeting between honest and responsible members of our different groups that we can really make a difference to our divided world.

The snag in dealing with any question like this is that as soon as it is dealt with, some other like Church unity crops up, and people feel that they have to move on to the new one. They may feel that once it's dealt with in the house-church or anywhere else that's that. We've had 'Time to Wake Up'—now it's time to go to sleep again. But such meetings make us realize that we must keep on caring about these questions and learn more and contribute more and gear them into our thinking about other problems. So representatives of our congregation have been attending every possible meeting that there has been in Leeds on the subjects of World Peace and Famine Relief, and our responsibility as citizens and so on, and the representatives have reported on these meetings to the congregation. We went to a big meeting about economic aid to under-developed countries, and so got connected to the West Riding Committee of War on Want; we went to a small meeting to think things over with the delegates from Buganda, and we have taken part in setting up the West Riding Council for African Affairs. If the Church doesn't make her witness, something will be missing in the attempts towards solving these questions. Surely we must believe that Christ has something to say through His Body, or else the Gospel has been delivered to us in vain. And it cuts the other way too: we see how these questions give vision and urgency to other questions that we thought were just ecclesiastical brain-teasers. Our meetings on 'Time to Wake Up' happened to come very close to our Week of Unity; we came to see that our disunity isn't just a personal inconvenience in the Church, it is a terrible thing for the world too, for it means that we are hindering Christ from using His Church to lead the world into unity and holiness with Himself. How can the world find its life in love with Christ if we Christians treat His Church as a series of competitive clubs? The delegates from Buganda were tremendously concerned that their country should not lose its soul in a whirl of economic development. The development will come—*now* is the time of revolution in Africa. What matters is whether there is a mature Church to pass on a gospel of grace, one that will stiffen the soul of twentieth-century Africa to cope with its coming twentieth-century body. Are we going to let Christ set His Church free to be a redeeming agency? Or are we going to say to Africa, 'You've had it: our throats are dry and our purses are empty and our imagination is dead'—why? Because we're still fighting a nineteenth-century battle with nineteenth-century tools and to-day is still a hundred years ahead of us.

In all this, our parish is on the edge of the edge, and so is this book. It ends in the middle of things, and we go on from here not knowing what may happen next. What is clear is that through the Church in the house God is making His people see who their friends ought to be and where they are, what to do about them and how.

Whatever is on the headlines of the newspaper, or in its leaders, must concern Church people. This concern can best come alive at the house level. As these groups develop more and more, the needs of the world and the needs of the parish will be united in a common concern, a common concern that the Body of Christ should extend the kingdom of God on earth, a common concern to link the local congregation to the parish community, and out and out to the uttermost part of the earth. Dr. Oldham teaches us that if we want to make a thing real we must make it local. This book is a plea to make the things of God local and real through the house-church.